ACTS

ACTS

EVERYDAY BIBLE COMMENTARY

Charles C. Ryrie

MOODY PUBLISHERS

CHICAGO

Interior design: Smartt Guys design
Cover design: Faceout Studio
Cover illustration of leaf pattern copyright © 2018 by Markovka / Shutterstock (74663932). All rights reserved.
Cover illustration of open book copyright © 2018 by IhorZigor / Shutterstock (185667422). All rights reserved.

Library of Congress Cataloging-in-Publication Data

Names: Ryrie, Charles Caldwell, 1925-2016, author.
Title: Acts / Charles Caldwell Ryrie.
Description: Chicago : Moody Publishers, 2018. | Series: Everyday Bible commentary series | Originally published: 1961. | Includes bibliographical references.
Identifiers: LCCN 2018010184 (print) | LCCN 2018013290 (ebook) | ISBN 9780802497253 () | ISBN 9780802418227
Subjects: LCSH: Bible. Acts--Commentaries.
Classification: LCC BS2625.53 (ebook) | LCC BS2625.53 .R97 2018 (print) | DDC 226.6/07--dc23
LC record available at https://lccn.loc.gov/2018010184

ISBN: 978-0-8024-1822-7

We hope you enjoy this book from Moody Publishers. Our goal is to provide high-quality, thought-provoking books and products that connect truth to your real needs and challenges. For more information on other books and products written and produced from a biblical perspective, go to www.moodypublishers.com or write to:

Moody Publishers
820 N. LaSalle Boulevard
Chicago, IL 60610

1 3 5 7 9 10 8 6 4 2

Printed in the United States of America

CONTENTS

PUBLISHER'S NOTE

For over sixty years, the Everyday Bible Commentary series (formerly titled Everyman's Bible Commentary series) has served millions of readers, helping them to grow in their understanding of both God and His Word. These commentaries—written by a host of evangelical scholars who are experts in their respective fields—provide biblical interpretation that is both accessible and rich, impacting the daily lives of Christians from diverse cultural and theological backgrounds.

So why rerelease the Everyday Bible Commentary series given its immense success? These commentaries have served readers tremendously well in generations past, and we want to ensure that they serve many more for generations to come. While these commentaries are not new, they remain relevant as the content in each volume provides timeless scriptural exposition. And perhaps today more than ever, Christians need reliable biblical instruction that has stood the test of time. With so many voices vying for our attention and allegiance, Christians need to understand the voice of the One calling out to us in Scripture so we may faithfully live for Him and His glory. And it is to this end that these commentaries were written: that believers may encounter God through His Word and embody it in their everyday lives.

BACKGROUNDS

....

THE IMPORTANCE OF THE BOOK

The historical importance of the book of Acts is unquestioned. It is the chief source book for the facts concerning Christianity in the first century after Christ. But the book is also important doctrinally, for in it are the seeds of doctrines developed later in the epistles—seeds that were nurtured in transformed lives. The doctrine of Acts is exemplified more in life than developed in systematic statement. It is doctrine in practice. Thus the book shows us what men can do in the power of the risen Savior. It is the record of the continuation of those things that Jesus began to do while on earth and that He carries on as risen Head of the church (1:1). The book furnishes us the principles for revival and missionary work; it shows the divine pattern for church government; and it exhibits not only steadfastness but expansion under persecution. It is a book for the church in any century.

THE AUTHOR OF THE BOOK

Dr. Luke was evidently a Greek and not a Jew, for in Colossians 4:12–14 he is distinguished from those who are said to be of the circumcision. His place of birth is unknown to us, though Antioch in Syria and Philippi are often suggested. Of necessity he would have had to receive his medical training in one of the three universities of the day—in Alexandria, Athens, or Tarsus. We know nothing of the circumstances of his conversion.

Although Luke is usually remembered as a physician, we should realize that he was primarily a missionary. His written ministry in the composition of the gospel of Luke qualifies him as such, but he also did itinerant missionary work. The Macedonian call was answered by Luke as well as Paul (16:13, 17). He was in charge of the work at Philippi for approximately six years, and later he preached in Rome (Philem. 24). He was also with Paul during his second missionary journey (2 Tim. 4:11).

THE DATE OF THE BOOK

Since the record in Acts concludes with Paul's arrival in Rome to begin his first confinement in that city, one would judge that the book was written about AD 63 in Rome during that first imprisonment. If it were written later it would be very difficult to explain why Luke did not mention such momentous events as the burning of Rome, the martyrdom of Paul, and the destruction of Jerusalem itself (particularly if it were written after AD 70).

THE AUTHORSHIP OF THE BOOK

Briefly, the proof for the Lucan authorship of Acts is usually developed along three lines: (1) The author of Acts was clearly a companion of Paul. This is seen from the "we" sections of the book—sections in which the first person plural is used signifying that the writer was a companion of Paul at those times (16:10–17; 20:5–21:18; 27:1–28:16). (2) By a process of elimination, that companion has to be Luke. The sections themselves eliminate, by mentioning, Silas, Timothy, Sopater, Aristarchus, Secundus, Gaius,

Tychicus, and Trophimus; while the prison epistles point to Luke's being the companion (Col. 4:14; Philem. 24). (3) The same man who wrote the "we" sections wrote the remainder of the book, for the style is the same. (4) This conclusion that Luke was the author is substantiated by the incidence of medical terms found in Acts (1:3, 3:7 ff.; 9:18, 33; 13:11; 28:1–10).

THE SOURCES OF THE BOOK

Luke's statement concerning his method of research is found in Luke 1:1–4. Since his purpose in the writing of both the gospel and the Acts was historical, and since his method was so careful, we may be assured that we have an accurate account of the events. In addition to all the care exercised by the author, the superintending work of the Holy Spirit guarantees the accuracy of the record that we have.

In producing his history of the apostolic age, Luke used several sources.

(1) Of some of the events he was a personal eyewitness. These are the "we" sections of the book; that is, sections in which Luke personally participated (16:10–17; 20:5–21:18; 27:1–28:31). These indicate that Luke was personally involved in the journey from Troas to Philippi (on the second missionary journey of Paul) and from Philippi (on the third journey) to Rome, including two years in Caesarea and two years in Rome. For all of these events he had his personal recollections and possibly diary-type written notes.

(2) Since Luke was with Paul during the five or six years before the writing of Acts, Paul could have provided him with information for the record in chapters 7, 9, 11:25–30, 13:1–16:8, and 17:1–20:4.

(3) Luke also had access to other eyewitnesses in gathering

his material—people like Silas, Timothy, Titus, Aristarchus, James, Philip and his daughters (19:29; 20:4; 21:8, 18; Col. 4:10; Philem. 24).

After gathering his facts Luke declares that he "investigated everything carefully" (Luke 1:3), that means that he sifted the facts before he wrote and that he made accurate use in his writing of those sifted facts. The physician's diagnostic skill was applied to the sifting of the source material in thorough preparation for writing an accurate historical account. And, of course, in all this work Luke was guided by the Holy Spirit of God so that the Acts is that exact historical record correct in every detail that God wanted us to have.

THE RISEN LORD

ACTS 1:1–26

....

It has often been said that the title of the Acts of the Apostles ought to be the Acts of the Risen Lord. The idea for such a change comes from the introduction to this first chapter (vv. 1–3). The former treatise (the gospel of Luke) that Dr. Luke wrote to Theophilus (apparently a noble convert to Christianity) had recorded the things that Jesus began to do while in His body of limitation. The present treatise (Acts) continued the record of the works of Jesus, only in His resurrection body in which He was seen by the apostles for forty days (v. 3). Three acts of this risen Lord are recorded in this chapter.

THE RISEN LORD CORRECTING, 1:4–7
Correction Concerning Service, 1:4–5
In His conversations with His disciples during the forty-day post-resurrection ministry, the Lord spoke concerning the kingdom of God. Apparently the disciples had become greatly enthused, and so the Lord cautioned them to wait in Jerusalem for the coming of the Holy Spirit before they began their service for Him. The ministry of the Spirit was not unknown to them; indeed they had experienced it (John 14:17; 20:22). But the baptizing

work of the Spirit was something they had not yet experienced, for the Lord said, "You will be baptized with the Holy Spirit not many days from now" (v. 5). Then they would be ready for service. (And, of course, after the promise had been received there would be no more need for tarrying.)

Correction concerning Seasons, 1:6–7

Jewish minds had long been agitated over the coming of Messiah's kingdom. When Jesus of Nazareth appeared on the scene of history, the hopes of many of the Jewish satellite people were pinned on Him. But these hopes were dashed against the stones of the hill of Calvary when their conquerors crucified their deliverer. Now that He had risen from the dead, their hopes were revived. "Will the kingdom come now?" was the burning question (v. 6). Questions about the kingdom are pertinent, the Lord implied, but as for answering the question about the time of the coming of the kingdom, this He could not do. To know many things about the kingdom is quite proper (v. 3), but "it is not for you to know times or epochs" (v. 7).

THE RISEN LORD COMMISSIONING, 1:8–11
The Nature of the Commission, 1:8

Until the kingdom should come, the disciples were commissioned to be occupied with witnessing of their Lord.

1. Its Power. The power of the commission is the person of the Holy Spirit who would come upon them and baptize them on the day of Pentecost.

2. Its Personnel. The commission is to be carried out by the disciples and all who are "My witnesses" (the correct rendering of "witnesses unto me" [KJV]).

3. Its Program. The commission's outreach is worldwide. In the

Acts the record of witnessing in Jerusalem is in chapters 1–7; in Judea and Samaria, 8–12; unto the uttermost part of the earth, 13–28.

The Need for the Commission, 1:9–11

The commission was given in view of the departure of the Lord. That ascension is described in verses 9 and 10 by three different verbs—"lifted up" (*epaireo*), "received" (*hupolambano*), and "was going" (*poreuomai*). As He ascended there appeared two angels who announced the promise of His return. They declared that the same person would return in like manner (that is, in clouds and great glory, Mark 13:26). This will be fulfilled in that future day when the Lord returns during the battle of Armageddon with His own to set up His millennial and eternal kingdom (Rev. 19:11–16; cf. Zech. 12:10; 14:14).

THE RISEN LORD CHOOSING, 1:12–26
The Necessity for the Choosing, 1:12–20

After the Lord had ascended, the disciples returned to Jerusalem from nearby Mount Olivet (less than one mile—a Sabbath day's journey). They assembled in the upper room, which many understand to have been in the house of Mary, the mother of John Mark. There were about 120 there altogether—including the remaining 11 apostles, Jesus' mother and brothers (who had not believed in Him until after the resurrection, John 7:5), and some other women. They continued in prayer and supplication during the ten days between Christ's ascension and the coming of the Spirit. As they did, Peter stood up and took charge of choosing a successor to Judas the betrayer. He reminded the group that the Old Testament Scriptures had predicted Judas's treachery (Ps. 41:9) and that they must now choose someone to take his place.

The Nature of the Choosing, 1:21–26

First Peter declared the qualifications necessary for an apostle. He must be a witness of the resurrection and a companion of the Lord during the whole of His public earthly ministry (vv. 21–22). Two candidates were nominated, Justus and Matthias. Then they prayed not for the Lord to choose but for the choice that the Lord had already made to be made known to them. The two names were put on lots, placed in an urn, and then the one that first fell from the urn was taken to be the Lord's choice. This was in accord with Old Testament practice (cf. Prov. 16:33) and is a method no longer needed by Christians with the coming of the abiding presence of the indwelling Spirit (Rom. 8:14; James 1:5). The lot fell on Matthias and from that time on he, not Paul, was considered as the twelfth apostle (cf. 2:14; 6:2). Apparently it will be Matthias who will be included in the fulfillment of such promises as Matthew 19:28 and Revelation 21:14 (though Paul is designated an apostle with authority equal to any of the Twelve).

PENTECOST—
BIRTHDAY OF THE CHURCH

ACTS 2:1–47

....

THE PROPHECY OF PENTECOST

Pentecost was a divinely planned event prophesied in Leviticus 23. The first of the annual feasts of Israel was Passover, which marked a new beginning for the children of Israel. This was a type of Christ our passover sacrificed for us (1 Cor. 5:7). The second was the feast of Unleavened Bread, which lasted for seven days and typified the lifelong walk of the believer in separation from evil. Firstfruits was the third feast, a type of the resurrection of Christ (John 12:24; 1 Cor. 15:23). This was followed fifty days later by the feast of Pentecost or, as it was sometimes called, the feast of Weeks because it fell seven (a week of) weeks after First-fruits. Likewise fifty days after the resurrection of Christ the event recorded in Acts 2 occurred.

THE POWER OF PENTECOST

The power of pentecost is a person, the Holy Spirit of God. Pentecostal power is simply the unhindered working of the Spirit in any life at any time. On the day of Pentecost He came to baptize the disciples into the body of Christ, thus welding them as a unit into the risen Head of the church (Acts 11:15–16; 1 Cor. 12:13). This is something that is experienced by each individual only once—at the time of his conversion. As other groups of believers were brought into the body of Christ they were baptized by the Spirit (Acts 11:15–16), but each individual experiences this only once (note the aorist tense of the verb in 1 Cor. 12:13). On the day of Pentecost the disciples were also filled with the Spirit (2:4), something that they and all believers may experience repeatedly (cf. 4:31; 6:5; 7:55; 9:17). At Pentecost, too, the Spirit inaugurated His permanent relationship of indwelling all believers in fulfillment of the Savior's promise recorded in John 14:17. In a very real sense Pentecost was the beginning of the age of the Spirit.

The Evidence of His Coming, 2:1–4

The coming of the Spirit was evinced by wind, fire, and tongues. Strictly speaking it was not wind but a roar or reverberation that filled the house. The literal translation of the phrase in verse 2 is "an echoing sound as of a mighty wind borne violently." The fire was really what the tongues looked like as they divided themselves over the company, a tongue settling upon the head of each one. Finally the disciples began each to speak in real languages new to the speakers and understood by those from various lands who were in Jerusalem for the feast of Pentecost. The natural sense of these verses indicates that the tongues were not jargon but real languages, and that the miracle was in the giving of the ability to speak these languages not in sensitizing in some way the ears of the hearers.

The Effects of His Coming, 2:5–13

Such startling and strange phenomena could not help but attract attention, and quickly a crowd gathered. Pentecost was one of the three festivals (along with Passover and Tabernacles) at which the law required attendance of Jews at the temple. Jerusalem was jammed. Indeed, 200,000 people could crowd together in the temple area alone. Jews from Babylonia, Syria, Egypt, Rome, Crete, and Arabia all heard of the wonderful works of God in their mother tongues.

At first the people were amazed (literally, wide-open astonishment, v. 7). Then they were perplexed or at a loss to understand what they were witnessing (v. 12). They knew that they did not know what was going on, and since ignorance is always a blow to man's pride, they were driven to criticism (v. 13). They concluded that the disciples were drunk (cf. Eph. 5:18).

THE PREACHING OF PENTECOST, 2:14–47
The Sermon, 2:14–36

As spokesman for the Twelve, Peter seized the opportunity, afforded by the charge of drunkenness leveled at the disciples, to preach Jesus to the crowd.

1. Introduction—explanation, 2:14–21. The message began with an explanation of the phenomena. It could not be drunkenness since it was only nine o'clock in the morning, and Jews engaged in the exercises of the synagogue on a feast day abstained from eating and drinking until 10 a.m. or even noon. It was not intoxication, Peter said; it was the ministry of the Spirit that caused the spectacle. To prove that the Spirit can produce such things, Peter quoted from Joel 2:28–32. This is a prophecy that will be fulfilled during the millennium when Israel is reestablished in her own land. Peter was not saying that the prophecy was fulfilled at Pentecost or even that it was partially fulfilled; knowing from Joel what the Spirit could do, he was simply reminding the Jews that they should have recognized what they were then seeing as a work of the Spirit also. He continued to quote from Joel at length only in order to be able to include the salvation invitation recorded in verse 21.

2. *Theme—Jesus is Messiah, 2:22-35.* To the English reader it means little to say that Jesus is Messiah or Christ. Jesus Christ to us is in the nature of first and last names, but to the Jews, Christ or Messiah was a well-defined concept from their Old Testament Scriptures and Jesus of Nazareth was to many merely another upstart human, religious teacher. To say that Jesus was the Christ was blasphemy. Thus Peter sought to prove to his audience that Jesus of Nazareth whom they knew well was their Messiah whom they also knew well. From Old Testament prophecies Peter reminded them of the picture of Messiah. From contemporary facts he painted a picture of Jesus. He superimposed these two pictures on each other to prove that Jesus is Christ, and the focal point of his entire argument was the resurrection.

First he proclaimed the resurrection of Jesus (vv. 22–24). Then he recalled the predictions of the resurrection from Psalm 16:8–11 (vv. 25–31). He showed that it was not David who was raised since he was still in a tomb; therefore, David must have been speaking about someone else, namely Messiah. "He looked ahead and spoke of the resurrection of the Christ" (v. 31a). Having proclaimed the resurrection of Jesus and having shown that Messiah had to be raised, Peter then reinforced his argument by citing proofs of the resurrection of Jesus (vv. 32–36). He reminded them that they were eyewitnesses of that miracle (v. 32), and we should remember that he was speaking to many residents of the city in which the resurrection had taken place less than two months before. Second, he cited the exaltation of Jesus at the right hand of God (vv. 33–35). This answered in the negative two questions: "Can a mere man occupy that place of honor?" and, "Can a dead man be exalted?" The third proof of the resurrection was the outpouring of the Holy Spirit—something no mere man, and certainly not a dead man, could do (vv. 33–35).

3. *Conclusion—Application, 2:36.* The pictures of Messiah and Jesus of Nazareth coincided. The proof of Jesus' resurrection was incontrovertible. Then Peter put it squarely to his audience to decide the truth of his message.

The Results, 2:37–47

1. *A Conviction, 2:37.* The word translated "pricked" (KJV) is a rare one and means to pierce, sting sharply, stun, smite. Outside the Scriptures it is used of horses dinting the earth with their hoofs. The hearts of the people had been smitten sharply by the preaching of the Word. This brought the question, "What shall we do?"

2. *A Change, 2:38–41.* Peter's answer was, "Repent, and each of you be baptized." This demanded a twofold change: first a change of mind and second a change of association. Change of mind is the meaning of the word repent. This is not mere sorrow for sin, though that may be involved; nor is it a mere mental assent to facts. It is the kind of basic change of mind that will result in a change of life and is perhaps best conveyed by the phrase "change of heart" (cf. Rom. 2:5, where lack of repentance is described as an "unrepentant heart"). For these people repentance meant a wholehearted change of mind about Jesus of Nazareth, thinking of Him no longer as merely the carpenter's son, a religious imposter, but now receiving Him as Lord (Divine) and Messiah.

The second part of the change concerned their association

as demonstrated by baptism. This was the visible proof of their repentance. It was not any sort of baptism (for baptism was well-known to these people both because of the ministry of John the Baptist and because it was one of the acts a Jewish proselyte had to undergo), but baptism in the name of Jesus Christ. Since baptism signifies association with the message, group, or person involved in authorizing it, baptism in the name of Jesus Christ meant for these people a severing of their ties with Judaism and an association with the messages of Jesus and His people. Baptism was the line of demarcation. Even today for a Jew it is not his profession of Christianity nor his attendance at Christian services nor his acceptance of the New Testament, but his submission to water baptism that definitely and finally excludes him from the Jewish community and marks him off as a Christian. This explains the insistence on the ordinance. Verse 41 implies that the 3,000 converts were all baptized on the same day, and this would have been quite possible with the number of pools and reservoirs in Jerusalem and with all 120 disciples helping. This baptism was "for the forgiveness of your sins" (v. 38). This does not mean in order that sins might be remitted, for everywhere in the New Testament sins are forgiven as a result of faith in Christ, not as a result of baptism. It means be baptized because of the remission of sins. The Greek preposition *eis,* for, has this meaning "because of" not only here but also in such a passage as Matthew 12:41 where the meaning can only be "they repented because of (not in order to) the preaching of Jonah." Repentance brought the remission of sins for this Pentecostal crowd, and because of the remission of sins they were asked to be baptized. (An excellent discussion of the Greek of verse 38 will be found in Robertson's *Word Pictures in the New Testament,* III, pp. 35–36.)

3. A Church, 2:42–47. Although the word *church* first appears in Acts at 5:11 (the word is not in the best manuscripts of 2:47), the fellowship formed at Pentecost was the first Christian church. It was characterized by four things. (1) The teaching of the apostles. This would have consisted largely of the rehearsal of the facts and meaning of the life of Jesus. (2) Fellowship. This means the sharing of their spiritual blessings in Christ and the sharing of their material substance. (3) Breaking of bread refers to the remembrance of the Lord in the Lord's Supper. (4) Prayers.

There were four results of this kind of fellowship. (1) Fear came upon every soul (v. 43 KJV). This is perfectly normal and healthy (I Peter 2:17). In this instance it was apparently encouraged by the miraculous signs that the apostles did. (2) Fellowship in material things was enjoyed by these early Christians (vv. 44–46). No doubt many of the pilgrims to the feast of Pentecost lingered in Jerusalem to learn more of their newfound faith in Christ, and this created pressing financial needs. After the incident recorded in chapter 5 there is no further mention of the use of this plan of sharing in common, for its necessity was undoubtedly short-lived. (3) Favor was enjoyed by the new group with all the people (v. 47). (4) Furtherance of the group was experienced as the Lord added daily such as were being saved (v. 47).

Pentecost is past. The church does not need another Pentecost. The Holy Spirit is here making available all His power. The need of the church is simply dedicated Christians who continue steadfastly in the apostles' doctrine, fellowship, breaking of bread, and prayers.

THE HEALING OF A LAME MAN

ACTS 3:1–26

....

One of the apostle's signs and wonders mentioned in 2:43 is described in detail in this chapter. This one was chosen because of its public nature and because of its relation to the progress of the early church.

THE MIRACLE, 3:1–11

Its Circumstances, 3:1–3

The circumstances surrounding this miracle were the crossing of two habits. The one was the habit of Peter and John in going (imperfect tense) to the temple; the other was the habit of the lame man to be carried (also imperfect) to the temple to beg. Even after the new church had been formed, the disciples continued to attend services at the temple (cf. 2:46).

Its Characteristics, 3:4–7

The miracle was unexpected (4–6a). It was alms for which the man was begging; it was healing that he received. The miracle was performed in the name of Jesus Christ (v. 6b). A name stands for all that the person is; therefore, the name of Christ includes all the power of Christ. The miracle was instantaneous (v. 7). The miracle was complete (v. 7). The man was not partially healed but completely so. The verb "were strengthened" is a medical term.

Its Consequences, 3:8–11

As a result of this miracle three things happened. First, the man was filled with joy. He leaped up as soon as he realized that his feet and ankle bones had been strengthened. Second, God received praise, for the man went into the temple with Peter and John praising God for what He had done. Apparently he recognized the source of the miracle. Third, there was a testimony to the people around. Here was a well-known character whom they had seen for years begging at the same stand; now he was walking and leaping. This caused such amazement among those who were at the temple that very quickly a crowd gathered in the colonnade at the eastern end of the south side of the temple area, the piazza known as Solomon's Porch (cf. John 10:23).

This miracle of physical healing is rightly seen as an illustration of spiritual healing. The lame man serves as an excellent picture of the helplessness and hopelessness of the sinner (cf. Rom. 5:6; Eph. 2:12) whose only hope is believing in the name of Jesus Christ (Acts 4:12). When one believes in Him, then instantaneously there is complete salvation, which brings joy to the sinner, praise to God, and a testimony to others.

THE MESSAGE, 3:12–26

The Introduction, 3:12

As on the day of Pentecost, Peter here used a current event or the healed man as an object lesson to introduce his message to the people who had gathered. He also rebuked them not for their surprise at what had occurred but for their lack of comprehension as to how it had happened—as if either John or himself were able to perform such a miracle.

The Theme, 3:13–18

As at Pentecost the theme of Peter's sermon was:

Jesus whom you killed is the Messiah. Almost as remarkable as the healing of the lame man is the transformation in Peter, for the same man who two months before had denied Jesus was now standing before some of the same crowd proclaiming Him. The theme of the sermon was developed by designating the Lord in five ways and making five statements about Him. The five designations were: (1) Servant (v. 13 rather than "Son"). This would immediately identify Jesus of Nazareth with the Servant-Messiah of the Old Testament (Isa. 42:1–9; 49:1–13; 52:13–53:12) and emphasized Peter's point that Messiah was not only a conquering ruler but a suffering servant (v. 18). (2) Jesus (v. 13) linked Messiah to the man of Nazareth who was only too well-known to this crowd. (3) and (4) The designations Holy and Righteous One asserted His equality with God and affirmed the deity of Jesus (v. 14). (5) Prince of life (v. 15), which means literally *author* or *leader of life* (cf. 5:31; Heb. 12:2 for the only other occurrences of the word).

The five statements about the Lord were these: (1) He is exalted (v. 13); (2) this is the same One who was delivered up by the people (v. 13); (3) He was falsely accused (vv. 13–14); (4) He was killed (v. 15); but (5) God raised Him from the dead and you know it (v. 15).

Peter then drawing all this together answered the original question—How was the lame man healed? It was His name through faith in His name (v. 16) that accomplished the miracle.

The Conclusion, 3:19–26

The only conclusion in view of the evidence was that it is imperative to repent. These Jews were asked to change their minds about Jesus and change their way of life by turning to the Lord. Peter promised that this would bring forgiveness of sins and the return of the Lord to establish the kingdom promised to Israel. (The words "in order that" in v. 19 should be translated by the phrase "that so.") For some this promise concerning the kingdom has posed a difficult problem; for they ask, "Would the kingdom have come then if these people had repented?" The answer need not be given, for the question is hypothetical since the plan of God left in no doubt the disposition of this offer by the people at that time. And yet it is true that the repentance of Israel will bring forgiveness of sins and the ushering in of the kingdom eventually. The phrase "times of refreshing" (v. 19) is evidently a synonym for the phrase "restoration of all things" (v. 21) or the millennial kingdom. But that kingdom will not come, apart from personal repentance. This was what the Jews rejected in Christ's ministry (cf. Matt. 4:17) and it was the same thing that they rejected in Peter's ministry on that day.

THE BEGINNING OF PERSECUTION

ACTS 4:1–37

....

Persecution was a blessing of the apostolic church. Five times in eleven years hands were stretched forth to vex the churches in Jerusalem. This chapter records the first of these persecutions with its resultant increase in power. It is the early thirties and the scene is Jerusalem.

THE PERSECUTION, 4:1–22

The Prison, 4:1–4

The opposition of the Pharisees is paramount in the Gospels. In the Acts it is the Sadducees who oppose the Christians. This is because the Sadducees disbelieved the doctrine of resurrection, which the apostles were preaching so powerfully. So intense was their hatred in this instance that they brought the high-ranking captain of the temple (v. 1) in on the arrest. However, although the message was a savor of death to them it was a savor of life to many others so that the total number of believers in Jerusalem increased to about five thousand (v. 4). This is the last time any such numbering is recorded.

The Preaching, 4:5–12

An august audience heard Peter's sermon on this occasion. Annas, the representative of Aaron in Jewish eyes and the real power in the priesthood; Caiphas, his son-in-law and the Roman appointed high priest (cf. John 15:24); John and Alexander, two notable persons; rulers, elders, and scribes were present. This was the spiritual aristocracy of Jerusalem, for they were the controlling and wealthiest of the priests. Their question was straightforward: how was the lame man healed?

The Spirit of God filling Peter spoke through him a message reported in ninety-two words of the Greek text, in which Peter turned the tables on the Sanhedrin and put them on trial. In this brief message he called attention first to the fact that the miracle was a good deed, not a crime (v. 9). Then he boldly stated that it took place in the name of the hated Nazarene for whose crucifixion they were responsible and from which death God raised Him (v. 10). He called attention to the fact that Messiah's rejection was predicted in the Old Testament (v. 11 cf. Ps. 118:22), and finally he offered salvation to them in that same name (v. 12).

The Punishment, 4:13–22

While Peter and John were absent, the Sanhedrin in conference recognized that since they could not deny the occurrence of the miracle their problem was to keep this doctrine of the resurrection of Jesus from spreading. So they charged Peter and John not to speak in His name anymore. The apostles' reply was simply: we must obey God and testify of what we have seen (vv. 19–20). "Uneducated and untrained" in verse 13 simply means untrained formally in the Rabbinic schools. "Having been with Jesus" in the same verse is probably to be understood as referring to their physical, not spiritual, companionship with the Lord particularly during the last week of His earthly life.

THE POWER, 4:23-37
Because of the Right Use of Prayer, 4:23–31

After being threatened, the disciples returned to their own group to pray. First, they addressed God as Lord (v. 24). This is not the usual word for Lord but the one from which comes the English word despot. It is used for the absolute relationship of a master to his slaves (cf. 1 Tim. 6:1–2; Titus 2:9; 1 Peter 2:18). Second, they showed their recognition of the power of God (v. 24b) particularly as it was displayed in the act of creation. Third, they submitted themselves to the plan of God (vv. 25–28). As they prayed, the Spirit opened to them the meaning of Psalm 2 as it applied to the crucifixion of Christ. The responsibility for that act is laid upon Herod, Pontius Pilate, Gentiles, and the people of Israel (v. 27); and the human responsibility is interwoven with the predetermined plan of God (v. 28). Fourth, they presented their petitions to God (vv. 29–30). Even in the stress of the situation their prayer was filled mainly with praise, not petition. But they did ask for one thing—boldness and boldness confirmed by miracles. They did not ask the Lord to remove the threats nor to relieve them of the problem, but to give them boldness to continue to testify and for confirmation of their message by signs and wonders.

The answer was given with another infilling of the Spirit, which was seen in this instance visibly by the shaking of their meeting place. And when they were filled again (as they had been on the day of Pentecost, 2:4) they spoke the Word with boldness.

Because of the Right Use of the Purse, 4:32–37

"Money talks!" And it did in the early church. The fellowship was strengthened and needs met by the voluntary agreement to hold things in common. This is not "Christian communism." The sale of property was quite voluntary (v. 34). The right of possession was not abolished. The community did not control the money until it had voluntarily been given to the apostles. The distribution was not made equally but according to need. These are not communistic principles. This is Christian charity in its finest display.

One of those who had a large part in this fellowship of goods was Barnabas. He was a Cypriot, evidently wealthy, called an apostle (14:14), and one whose spiritual gift was exhortation (cf. 11:23). But here he is an outstanding example of the love of Christ ruling the heart and displaying itself in caring for other believers.

PURITY, PURGING, AND PERSECUTION

ACTS 5:1–42

....

PURITY, 5:1–11

For the time is come that judgment must begin at the house of God (1 Peter 4:17). Satan had been unsuccessful in his attempts to thwart the message of the resurrection by attacking the church from without; so he attacked from within. But God intervened to preserve the purity of the testimony by purging out the weak members of the group. Sometimes subtraction is better than addition.

The Occasion

Barnabas's generosity was undoubtedly applauded in the church. This set Ananias and Sapphira to thinking. They too had some real estate and they wanted acclaim. So they sold the property and agreed simply to pretend that they were giving all that they had received for it to the church. Their sin was hypocrisy. No regulation required them to give the entire sum; but honesty in whatever they did decide to do was required. They simply pretended greater devotedness to Christ than they actually had, and for this they were judged.

The Operation

God operated and cut out this cancer in the group. Peter was the means used by God, not to call down judgment, but to point out the sin. He diagnosed it as a sin against the Holy Spirit (vv. 3, 9), which God judged by physical death. All sin is judged though God may not choose to do it always in the same manner. Heaven's silence is not heaven's consent, and God hates sin in His people just as much today as when He demonstrated His hatred in this instance. Neither is physical death an uncommon punishment for sin in New Testament times (cf. 1 Cor. 11:30; 1 John 5:16).

The Outcome

There were three immediate results of this purging. First, the purity of the church was preserved intact. Second, a wholesome, godly fear pervaded the group (v. 11). It was a dangerous thing to be a follower of Christ unless one was willing to walk straight. Third, new power was experienced by the believers. Signs and wonders were performed and many people were added to the Lord, "multitudes of men and women" (v. 14). Nothing will sap the power of a church's testimony more quickly than pews filled with sinning Christians. There is no substitute for personal purity but it costs to attain it.

PERSECUTION, 5:12–42
The Prelude, 5:12–16

Certain events within and outside the church led to the second persecution. One was the miracle working power of the apostles. This authenticated the message and drew fire from the

Sadducees. Another was the accord of the believers (v. 12) that set the Christians apart. A third was the growing number being added to the Christian group. This alarmed the Jewish leaders.

The Prison, 5:17–21a

Again it was the Sadducees who, enraged by the preaching of the resurrection, had the apostles cast into prison. Evidently they planned to gather in council the next morning to examine and punish the apostles. But God had other plans, and sent an angel of the Lord to open the prison and command them to do again the very thing that had gotten them imprisoned. The apostles' full obedience is startling, for early in the morning they were in the temple again preaching.

The Preaching, 5:21b–39

When the Sanhedrin sent for the prisoners, they found none. But someone told them that the prisoners were free and teaching in the temple again. So upon recapturing them they charged them with two things: first, disobedience to their previous order not to teach in the name of Jesus, and, second, planning to charge the Sanhedrin with the death of Jesus (v. 28). To this Peter simply replied that obedience to God took priority over obedience to man (v. 29), and then he took the opportunity to present the message once again to them. "Those who obey Him" in verse 32 is not some special group of believers to whom the Spirit is given but all who have obeyed by believing (cf. Rom. 1:15). The effect on the hearers was one of rage, not repentance (v. 33).

On the previous night in jail God used supernatural means to deliver the apostles. Now He used natural means—the counsel of one of the most celebrated teachers of the law, Gamaliel, to prevent any harm coming to the apostles. Gamaliel was a Pharisee and may have been motivated only by the desire to keep the Sadducees from gaining the point. At any rate his suggestion was: "Hands off." He suggested dodging the issue whereas he might have suggested investigating the claims of the message. He recalled two previous movements—that of Theudas and that of Judas—which petered out because they were not of God, and he concluded that this Jesus movement would do likewise if it were not.

The Punishment, 5:40–42

The Sanhedrin agreed, but nonetheless had the apostles beaten for their disobedience to their previous command (cf. Deut. 25:2–3). Then they released the apostles, who departed rejoicing that they were worthy to suffer for their Lord and who continued daily to preach and teach Christ both in private homes and in the temple. These were men with singleness of purpose—to obey the great commission of their risen Lord.

WORKERS TOGETHER
WITH GOD

ACTS 6:1–7

....

The Reasons, 6:1–2, 4

Widows had always received particular attention from God in the legislation of the Old Testament. Many of them had believed in Christ and became then the responsibility of the new church. Some were Hellenistic Jews (that is, they had originally come from countries outside of Palestine and spoke Greek) and others were Palestinian Jews (who spoke Hebrew and observed all the customs of Judaism). The former group charged that their widows were being neglected in the daily distribution of the relief money. Legitimate or not, the charge was one of the reasons for needing additional workers.

Coupled with that was the increasing burden of the work that had fallen on the apostles. They could not continue to minister the Word and minister relief to the widows, so they suggested the appointment of new workers to assume some of the load.

The Requirements, 6:3

Five qualifications were required. (1) These helpers were to be men. The Greek word used is the specific one that means males. (2) They had to be believers—"among you." No outsiders were to have part in the government of the church. (3) They had to be reputable. This is the meaning of "of good reputation." Public testimony had to certify their sterling character (cf. 1 Tim. 3:7; 5:10; Titus 1:6). (4) They had to be spiritual—"full of the Spirit." This was the normal, not unusual, expectation of the church. (5) They had to be wise. This involves native intelligence as well as the wisdom of the Spirit.

The Results, 6:5–7

The multitude, pleased at the requirements set forth by the apostles, chose seven men. The names of all seven are Greek, and although it does not necessarily prove that they were all Hellenistic Jews, it does show that they were chosen in the interest of the Hellenists who had lodged the complaint. The apostles directed, but the multitude chose. Then the seven were ordained; that is, the apostles laid their hands on them as a sign of their association with them in the work (cf. Lev. 3:2). The apostles identified themselves with the work of the seven through this act.

As a result the Word of God increased (v. 7) simply because the apostles had more time to devote to it. Too, many were added to the church including a company of priests.

Usually this passage is understood to record the choosing of the first deacons since the word "serve" in verse 2 is the verb from which we get the noun deacon. However, it is a question whether the word is being used in a technical sense to indicate the establishment of the office of deacon or whether the word is being used in a general sense of those who serve as it is frequently in Acts (cf. 1:17, 25; 6:1, 4; 11:29; 12:25; 19:22; 20:24; 21:19). Perhaps these seven should be called helpers rather than official deacons, though the office of deacon had clearly developed by the time of Paul's first imprisonment (Phil. 1:1).

THE FIRST MARTYR

ACTS 6:8–8:1a

....

O ur attention is now turned to one of those seven helpers, Stephen. His name means, appropriately, crown, for he was the first to wear the martyr's crown. Too, he was the historical link between Peter and Paul, for it is at Stephen's stoning that Paul is first mentioned.

THE STIRRING OF THE PEOPLE, 6:8–7:1

Stephen was a "deacon" to whom God also gave the responsibility of ministering the Word and whose ministry was confirmed by signs and wonders. Apparently his ministry was particularly among the Hellenistic Jews in Jerusalem who according to verse 9 may have had as many as five synagogues. By some means these unbelieving Jews were able to stir up the people and they accused Stephen before the Sanhedrin. The charge was twofold: (1) Stephen was speaking against the temple and (2) he was changing the law of Moses. The charge also labeled him as a blasphemer. As he prepared to answer, the Sanhedrin saw his face shining as the face of an angel (cf. Ex. 34:29; 2 Cor. 3:18).

THE SERMON OF STEPHEN, 7:2–53

This is the longest sermon recorded in the book of Acts. It is as long as the three of Paul's together, and it is an able defense for the claims of Jesus Christ (although His name is not used and He is referred to only in v. 52). The text of the message is found in verse 51: "you are doing just as your fathers did." Stephen proved this point by citing the simple facts of Jewish history and climaxing with the contemporary rejection of Jesus.

Stephen first cited the history of Abraham (vv. 2–8), for to him all Jews looked and to him the promise concerning the seed was given. Stephen then passed to Joseph (vv. 9–16) possibly because Joseph is such a good type of Christ. He was sold because of envy (cf. Mark 15:10) but God was with him (cf. Acts 10:38); there was a famine, which pictured Israel's condition at that time; and it was the second time when Joseph was revealed to his brethren just as it will be at our Lord's second coming that Israel will recognize Him.

Then Stephen spoke of Moses (vv. 17–38). The charge that had been leveled at him concerned his relationship to Moses. He pointed out how Moses, the deliverer, had been rejected by his own people at first, and how Moses prophesied concerning Christ who was to come (v. 37). (Note that the word translated "congregation" in v. 38 should be translated "assembly." This is the non-technical use of the word and in no way implies that the church existed in Old Testament times.) But even after Moses, the apostasy continued (vv. 39–53). While Moses was receiving the law, the people were making a gold calf (v. 41). They worshiped the hosts of heaven, Moloch and Remphan (vv. 42–43). This brought him to the time of Solomon and his temple, and since he had been accused of defaming the temple he reminded his audience that God does not dwell in temples made by men (cf. 1 Kings 8:27; Isa. 66:1–2).

Finally Stephen applied his message to the Sanhedrin. You, he said, are doing the same as your forefathers by rejecting God's message through Jesus. This, he charged, was a sin against the Holy Spirit, and he laid the blame for the slaying of Christ squarely on them (v. 52).

THE STONING OF STEPHEN, 7:54–8:1a

As Stephen bore down with the truth, the members of the council began to murmur and become disorderly. Finally, under so much conviction of heart, they interrupted his defense and rushed on him in preparation for stoning. So angered were they at him that they literally gnashed their teeth like ravenous beasts, stopped their ears so as not to hear him, cast him out of the city, and stoned him. There was no vote or recognition of the fact that the Sanhedrin did not of itself have the power of sentencing to death.

Amid all this confusion stood the serene figure of Stephen, sustained by the risen Lord standing on the right hand of God. This position indicates His ministry as a Melchizedekan priest giving sustenance to His people (cf. Gen. 14:18). Christ's work of redeeming is finished—thus in this respect He is seated; but His work of sustaining His own goes on—in this respect He is standing. And as the stoning proceeded, Stephen kneeled and asked the Lord to receive his spirit and not to lay this sin to the charge of the Jews (cf. Luke 23:34). (This is a rare example of a prayer directed to the second person of the Trinity.) Then he fell asleep and was ushered immediately in the presence of his Savior.

But the story does not end there. The first sentence of the next chapter completes it. Stephen was dead, but God's work lived on and would soon be carried on through the life of the man Saul who was standing by holding the witnesses' clothes and consenting to Stephen's death. Out of seeming tragedy came new advance. Out of Stephen came Paul.

ENFORCED
EXPANSION

ACTS 8:1–40

....

The Great Commission was not confined to Jerusalem but included Judea, Samaria, and the uttermost part of the earth. The means God used to spread the good news beyond Jerusalem was the fourth persecution (vv. 1–4) with its resultant witness in Samaria (vv. 5–25) and on the Gaza road (vv. 26–40).

THE PERSECUTION IN JERUSALEM, 8:1–4

In Jerusalem opinion was evidently divided over the justice of the death of Stephen. Some devout Jews were not so sure that the right thing had been done and they saw to his burial (v. 2). For others his death only whetted their vindictive appetites, and they intensified persecution of the Christians. This time, however, the apostles were not directly attacked; only the disciples were scattered. One of the chief persecutors, and the man who now begins to dominate the book of Acts, was Saul. The intensity of his attacks is shown by the fact that he went into the homes, that he included women, and that he saw to it that they were imprisoned. Beating and loss of property would have unavoidably been included. According to 11:19 those who were scattered went as far as Phoenicia, Cyprus, and Antioch.

THE PREACHING IN SAMARIA, 8:5–25

Another deacon, Philip, is now brought to our attention. He went to Samaria to preach Christ. One of those who heard was Simon, a sorcerer who had deceived the people with his claims. He too believed (v. 13) and was baptized. However, his faith was evidently not unto salvation (cf. v. 19 and James 2:14–20), for he apparently only believed that Jesus was a great power from God and he did not receive Him as his Savior. He believed facts about Jesus but did not transfer his trust to Him.

When the apostles in Jerusalem heard what had happened, they sent Peter and John to verify the report. When they laid their hands on the Samaritans, the gift of the Spirit that the Jews had received at Pentecost was imparted to the Samaritans as well; and Simon, seeing this great miracle, offered to buy this power thinking it would enhance his sorcery. But Peter discerned the true state of his heart and besought him truly to repent of his wickedness.

Why was the gift of the Spirit delayed until the coming of Peter and John? To answer this we must recall who the Samaritans were. They were half-caste Jews (cf. 2 Kings 17:24; Ezra 4; Neh. 6; John 4) who had their own rival worship system. "Jews have no dealings with Samaritans" (John 4:9). If the Spirit had been given to the Samaritans while Philip was preaching, then the Samaritans might well have thought that their brand of Christianity was distinct from the Judean brand just as their existing worship was distinct from Judaism. Thus there would have been two churches. But by the laying on of hands of Peter and John, apostles from Jerusalem, in the giving of the Spirit, God assured unity in the infant church. The Samaritan movement was identified with that of Judea. In the house of Cornelius (cf. 10:44) there was no delay in order to prove to the Jews present that Gentiles were coming into the church on an equal basis with them.

THE PREACHING ON THE GAZA ROAD, 8:26–29

Gaza was originally a fortress city on the road to Egypt. In 96 BC, it was utterly destroyed, and although a new city was built nearby, the road to Egypt ran through the old fortress, which was left in ruins. Traveling on this road was an official of the Queen of Ethiopia (all of Africa south of Egypt) who, evidently as a proselyte of the gate (Deut. 23:1), had been to Jerusalem to worship. On the return trip he was reading Isaiah as he met Philip.

Philip's steps were definitely ordered of the Spirit. Engaged in a most successful evangelistic work in Samaria, the Spirit commanded him to interrupt it and go to the Gaza road (v. 26). Because Philip obeyed, the Spirit directed his next move, which was to join himself to the Ethiopian's chariot (v. 29). How many other chariots passed previously we do not know, but it was not until Philip had explicit leading that he moved from the side of the road. But when told to speak to the Ethiopian, Philip was bold to invade his privacy and wisely speak to him from the Scripture that he was engaged in reading. He showed the man that Isaiah was speaking of Christ who was the Jesus of Nazareth of whom the Ethiopian had heard a great deal in Jerusalem. Philip apparently also instructed him concerning baptism, for as soon as they saw water the Ethiopian requested baptism. (Verse 37 is not in best manuscripts.) After this the Spirit caught Philip away to Azotus, which is Ashdod, and Philip continued preaching as he made his way north to Caesarea where he eventually made his home (21:28). Though Philip himself did not personally leave Palestine, yet because of this sensitivity to the leading of the Spirit, the gospel had now gone to Ethiopia, one of the uttermost parts.

10

THE CONVERSION OF PAUL

ACTS 9:1–31

....

With the introduction of the man who dominated the narrative from this point on, we reach a turning point in the book of Acts. This chapter is the first of three accounts of Paul's conversion in Acts (cf. 22:1–16; 26:9–18).

THE CONVERSION, 9:1–9

Paul was a determined man whose very life breath was "breathing threats and murder against the disciples of the Lord." He was like a warhorse who had the scent of battle (for the verb is literally breathing *in*) and who was looking for new fields to conquer. He cast his eyes to the north where lay Damascus and a large group of Christians. Perhaps some had been in Jerusalem for Pentecost and had returned with the news of the events of that day. Those who believed had not been persecuted, for they had not even been forced to separate from the synagogues (22:12). But Paul had in mind changing all that, so he asked for authority from the high priest in Jerusalem to bring any Damascus Christians to Jerusalem for trial.

God had other plans. Four things stand out in this account of Paul's conversion.

First, it is evident from the Lord's words "it is hard for thee to kick against the pricks" (KJV) that in his innermost soul Paul was under conviction. He was trying to stifle the goading of his conscience by increasing the intensity of his persecution.

Second, there was conversion. As the voice from heaven asked, "Why do you persecute Me?" it began to dawn on Paul that Jesus of Nazareth was the Messiah and Lord. And this life-changing truth was confirmed to him when the Lord said, "I am Jesus whom you are persecuting." In that moment when he recognized Jesus as his Messiah and placed his faith in Him, Paul became a new man in Christ.

Third, there was consecration. Paul was one of those rare persons who settled the matter of life service at the same time as he settled the question of the salvation of his soul (cf. 1 Sam. 3:9). When he asked, "What wilt thou have me to do?" (KJV) he was offering the Lord all his life for service without reservation (cf. 22:10).

Fourth, there was communion or fellowship during the three days he was without sight, food, and water.

THE CHRONOLOGY, 9:10–31
Damascus, 9:10–22

On the scene appeared one of whom nothing is previously recorded and who disappears from the record almost as soon as he appears (cf. 22:12). Ananias to whom the Lord appeared was God's instrument in Paul's infant Christian life. After being assured by the Lord that Paul was a changed man (vv. 13–16) Ananias immediately went to the house of Judas in Straight Street, Damascus, to minister to Paul in the matters of his sight, his baptism, his filling with the Spirit, his physical need for food, and communion in the things of the Lord. After some days Paul began to preach Christ in the synagogues of Damascus. The people couldn't believe what they heard, for here was the arch-persecutor now preaching the faith that he had set out to destroy.

Arabia, Galatians 1:17

In this passage Paul reveals the fact that immediately after his conversion he spent three years in Arabia before going to Jerusalem to see the apostles. This extended period of time is referred to in Acts apparently only by the phrase "when many days had elapsed" (9:23). To what specific spot in Arabia the apostle went we do not know, but it may have been a deserted place or it may well have been to one of the cities to the south of Palestine. Neither are we given any clue as to how he spent his time there, but evidently he was reorienting himself and his theology in the light of the Damascus Road experience. In addition to all of Paul's previous thorough training in the rabbinical school of Gamaliel, God considered that he still needed three more years before he was fully prepared for service.

Damascus, 9:23–25

Paul's testimony in the synagogues of Damascus was even more powerful after his Arabian sojourn—so much so that the Jews plotted against his life; and had the disciples not helped him escape by letting him over the city wall in a basket, presumably he would have been slain.

Jerusalem, 9:26–29 (cf. Gal. 1:18–19)

When Paul came to Jerusalem, the disciples were afraid of him, still fearing that he was not really a follower of the Lord.

But Barnabas vouched for him, and he remained there about fifteen days, witnessing particularly to the Hellenistic Jews (with whom Paul had cooperated in the death of Stephen) with such effectiveness that again his life was in jeopardy.

Tarsus, 9:30–31

When the plot was discovered, the disciples took Paul to the seaport, Caesarea, and he went home to Tarsus. He was probably there nearly ten years before he was called to help Barnabas in the work at Antioch. This must have been a very difficult time, for the one who had gone away as a promising rabbinical student had now returned as a despised Christian.

11

GENTILES IN THE CHURCH

ACTS 9:32–11:18

....

THE PREPARATION OF THE MESSENGER
Peter the Leader, 9:32–43

The action returns again to Peter who was visiting the churches in Palestine, which were having good growth (v. 31). When he came to Lydda he was used in the healing of Aeneas who had been paralyzed for eight years and who apparently was an unbeliever. Since Aeneas's paralytic condition was well-known in the region, his miraculous healing became the means of causing many to turn to the Lord.

Meanwhile, at nearby Joppa on the coast, a female disciple, Dorcas, who had spent her days doing good works in making clothes for the needy, died. When the disciples heard that Peter was only ten miles away in Lydda, they sent for him. When he came he found the widows (probably those who had received clothes from Dorcas) weeping in the upper chamber where her body had been laid. Peter, in imitation of the Lord's actions in the house of Jairus (Matt. 9:25), asked them all to leave and having prayed he commanded Dorcas to come to life. When she saw

Peter she sat up, he offered her help, and he presented her alive to the waiting people. This, too, became known in the vicinity, and like the healing of Aeneas it was the cause of many turning to the Lord. And Peter remained there as the guest of Simon the tanner.

Peter the Learner, 10:1–22

The scene now shifts to Caesarea, twenty-seven miles up the coast where we are introduced to a distinguished centurion who commanded the hundred men of the Italian band. He, of course, was a Gentile, but a very devout one. Probably he was a proselyte of the gate; that is, he believed in the God of Judaism and His government, but had not yet taken any of the steps to become a full-fledged proselyte. He was a generous and prayerful man (v. 2). However, he was not yet a saved man (cf. 11:14) even though he was very religious.

As he was praying one day, an angel of God appeared and told him to send for Peter in Simon the tanner's house in Joppa. Immediately, doubting nothing, Cornelius sent two of his servants to Joppa.

The next day when the messengers were nearing Joppa, Peter, waiting for the noon meal, was on the flat roof of Simon's house praying. He fell into a trance and saw a great sheet full of all sorts of ceremonially unclean animals being let down from heaven. Suddenly a voice commanded: "Get up, Peter, kill and eat!" Peter apparently recognized the order as from the Lord, but he did not acknowledge the Lord's right to command him to do what was forbidden by the Mosaic law. His reply was in the form of a great contradiction: "By no means, Lord." If He is Lord one cannot say, "By no means," and if one says, "By no means," He cannot be Lord. But God assured him that He had cleansed these animals, and repeated the action three times. At this point Cornelius's servants appeared, and since the Lord had told Peter that he should go with them, he did. All the time he was pondering the meaning of the vision, which was simply that unclean Gentiles were now to be cleansed by the gospel of Christ and brought into the church on the same basis as Jewish believers.

THE PREACHING OF THE MESSAGE, 10:23–11:18

When they arrived in Caesarea, Cornelius was waiting for them with his relatives and friends. What faith Cornelius displayed in calling together these people to hear someone he had been told to send for in a vision speak some strange message to them! It was the third day since the vision of the sheet full of unclean animals, but during those days Peter had comprehended what God was trying to say to him about the Gentiles' coming into the blessings of the gospel (v. 28). Thus the message was first preached to them in the house of Cornelius.

Peter began by declaring that he now understood that God was no respecter of persons, a fact that the Old Testament affirms repeatedly (cf. Deut. 10:17; Job 34:19; 2 Chron.19:7). God's message to all peoples is peace by Jesus Christ (v. 36). Then the essential facts of the life and death of Christ were stated—He proved Himself by His life (v. 38), He was crucified (v. 39), He was raised and seen by predetermined witnesses (vv. 40–41), and He will someday judge the living and the dead (v. 42). Then Peter invited these Gentiles ("everyone") to believe in Him and receive remission of sins (v. 43).

Apparently Peter did not really finish his message, for as he was speaking the Spirit fell upon these people who believed the message, and they spoke in tongues giving evidence of the Spirit's coming. This, of course, completely astonished the Jewish brethren with Peter (note that Peter had wisely taken along witnesses, cf. v. 23), for this clearly meant that God had received these Gentiles into the fellowship not only on an equal basis with the Jews but entirely apart from the laying on of Jewish hands. The Spirit's coming at the moment of salvation is the normal pattern as seen here in the conversion of the Gentiles, and the gift of tongues was the sign to the Jews present of God's working. Water baptism followed and Peter and the others remained a few days with the new converts. It must have been a time of very happy and precious fellowship enjoying their oneness in Christ.

But all were not happy over these Gentile converts. The brethren in Jerusalem heard what had happened and they accused Peter of violating Jewish law by eating with uncircumcised Gentiles. They had not yet learned the lesson of the sheet filled with unclean animals but still considered Christianity to be exclusively for Jewish believers. So Peter rehearsed for them the events of the previous days (11:1–18). He told them of the great sheet, of the baptizing work of the Spirit on Gentiles just as He had done for them at Pentecost (vv. 15–16), and mentioned the presence of the six Jewish brethren he had taken with him to Caesarea. Then he simply rested his case by asking, If God so obviously did for Gentiles what He has done for us, who was I to stand in God's way? (v. 17). When the leaders heard these facts, they too glorified God for having given eternal life to the Gentiles. The first test had been successfully passed, but the church was to deal again with this problem of Jewish-Gentile relations (ch. 15).

THE CHURCH AT ANTIOCH

ACTS 11:19–30

....

THE FOUNDING OF THE CHURCH, 11:19–21

Luke now returns to the persecution of Stephen and the scattering of the disciples that followed it. They were driven as far as Phenice (Phoenicia—where Tyre and Sidon are located), Cyprus, and Antioch, and their preaching was restricted to Jews only. Probably the events recorded here preceded in point of time the preaching in the house of Cornelius so that those who were scattered had not heard that God was now including Gentiles in His program. Many Jews who heard believed and turned to the Lord.

THE FURTHERING OF THE CHURCH, 11:22–26

The word of the conversion of these people got back to Jerusalem, which, because of seniority, location, and connection with the apostles, continued to be the "mother church." Barnabas was dispatched to see what was going on. He was likely chosen because he was a Hellenist as were many of these new converts and he was a Cypriot as were many of the preachers. He also possessed the spiritual qualities necessary for such a ministry, for he was a good man (void of any censuring spirit), full of the Spirit and of faith. Coming to Antioch he saw the grace of God in the changed lives of the believers (cf. 13:12 for another example of doctrine in action) and exhorted them to cleave to the Lord. He also saw that a second person would be necessary to help carry on the work there properly and so he sent for Saul in Tarsus. It is possible that the apostles in Jerusalem had authorized Barnabas to send for Saul even before Barnabas had left Jerusalem since it seemed to be their custom to send two people on such missions (cf. 8:14). At any rate both of them ministered in the church for a year teaching and exhorting the people.

It was in Antioch that the disciples were first called Christians. The word appears in the New Testament only here, Acts 26:28, and 1 Peter 4:16. It was not a term that God gave them nor that they bestowed upon themselves, but one with which the Gentiles dubbed them (for it would be very unlikely that Jews would have used any name with Christ in it). The word means a partisan of Christ or one who belongs to Christ's party. Thus the work was furthered through the proper exercise of gifts in the ministries of Barnabas and Saul and through the distinct marking off of the believers by their new name.

THE FUNCTIONING OF THE CHURCH, 11:27–30

Soon the church had an opportunity to minister in material things in return for the spiritual ministry they had received. Prophets from Jerusalem came to Antioch, and Agabus, one of them, prophesied of a famine to come (which occurred in the days of Claudius, whose entire reign (AD 41–54) was plagued with shortages). When the church heard of it they not only believed the prophecy but acted by collecting and sending to Jerusalem relief money. Barnabas and Saul were chosen to carry this benevolence and they are called elders. This is the first use of this word in Acts though the office was undoubtedly a carryover from the organization of the synagogue, without any formal institution in the church. It is worthy of notice that this dispensing of money was entrusted only to these high officers in the church, and that it was considered important enough to send away the two outstanding teachers in the church.

THE HERODIAN
PERSECUTION

ACTS 12:1–25

....

THE DEVILMENT OF HEROD, 12:1

For the fifth time now the church in Jerusalem was plagued with persecution. First it was by the Sadducees, elders, rulers, and scribes (ch. 4). Then it was from the Sadducees alone because of the preaching of the resurrection (ch. 5). Third, those of the synagogue of the Libertines brought Stephen to trial (ch. 6). Along with this Saul headed the intense persecution of the church at Jerusalem so that all but the apostles were scattered (ch. 8). This fifth persecution was instigated by Herod about the same time that Paul and Barnabas were visiting the churches in Judea (11:29–30). This Herod was Herod Agrippa I, grandson of Herod the Great who was ruling at the time of the birth of Christ. He was a man who had cultivated the good will of the Jews by observing their customs and preferring their company. He is described in secular sources as a mild, liberal, yet ambitious ruler.

THE DEATH OF JAMES, 12:2

In order further to court the favor of the Jews, Herod had James the brother of John killed. This son of Zebedee was decapitated in fulfillment of the Lord's prophecy in Mark 10:39. It is interesting to note that of these two inseparable brothers one was the first apostle to die and the other was, as far as we know, the last.

THE DELIVERANCE OF PETER, 12:3–19

When Herod saw that the slaying of James pleased the Jews, he proceeded to extend his persecution of the church by seizing Peter. The time was Passover, 14th to 21st Nisan, Easter time, and the year was the year of Herod's death, AD 44. But Herod did not want to kill Peter until after Passover since the Jews would have been occupied with the rituals of Passover and less able to appreciate fully what he was doing for them.

In the meantime the church was praying, and in answer to their prayers God delivered him the night before his planned execution. But Peter was sleeping that night! Undoubtedly he remembered the promise of the Lord that he would live to be an elderly man (John 21:18). The deliverance was accomplished by an angel of the Lord and in the face of the strictest precautions Herod could take. Two chains and four soldiers (two by Peter's side and two at the door) were supposed to keep him safe for the executioner. Herod remembered what had happened before when Peter was in jail (5:19), and he didn't want a repeat performance. But the power of God is greater than that of any Herod, and the chains fell off, the doors of the prison were opened, and Peter thought he was seeing a vision. This is most natural particularly in view of his recent experience, with the vision of the great sheet.

However, when he came to himself he realized what had happened (v. 11). Then a very real problem faced him—where should a marked man go? He decided to go first where the church was gathered praying to let them know of his deliverance. So he went to the house of Mary the mother of John Mark. The damsel who answered the door left him standing there while she ran to tell the others who could not believe that their prayers were being answered and thought it was Peter's angel (or spirit). Peter had to continue knocking, and when he finally convinced them that it was he, he related how the Lord had delivered him. Then he thought of his personal safety and departed into hiding in an unnamed place. Of course, when the news got out that Peter was gone someone had to pay, and it was the soldiers who had been assigned to guard him who paid with their lives. Thus the fifth persecution ended in death for one (James) and deliverance for another (Peter). Inscrutable are the ways of God.

THE DESTRUCTION OF HEROD, 12:20–23

After the deliverance of Peter, Herod went to Caesarea. While there an attempt was made at reconciliation between Herod and the chief cities of Phoenicia, Tyre and Sidon. The cause of the trouble is unknown, but although Tyre and Sidon were free cities under the Romans they had to maintain good relations with Herod since they were economically dependent on Herod's territory. Blastus, the king's chamberlain, was their intermediary and a reconciliation was evidently effected. The public announcement of this was apparently made on a festival day (perhaps the anniversary of the Emperor's birthday). The people responded by shouting, "The voice of a god and not of a man!" Forthwith an angel of the Lord smote him because he did not repudiate the acclamation and thus did not give God His glory. Josephus says that Herod was immediately seized with violent internal pains and that he lingered in agony for five days before he finally died.

THE DISSEMINATION OF THE WORD, 12:24–25

In contrast to the persecutor's miserable demise, the Word of God flourished (cf. 6:7; 9:31). Persecution only promoted the Word. In the meantime Paul and Barnabas had fulfilled their mission of bringing the famine relief money to the churches in Judea, so they returned to Antioch taking with them John Mark.

THE FIRST
MISSIONARY JOURNEY

ACTS 13:1–14:28

Chapter 13 marks a major dividing point in the book of Acts. The first twelve chapters have recorded the events of the spread of Christianity in Jerusalem and Judea and Samaria (except 11:19–30). Now the third part of the Great Commission begins to be fulfilled, and the gospel is taken to the uttermost part of the earth. Whereas 1–12 traced the progress of the message from Jerusalem to Antioch, 13–28 records the movement from Antioch to Rome.

EVENTS IN ANTIOCH, 13:1–4

The church at Antioch was blessed with a number of outstanding leaders. Barnabas and Saul had previously been mentioned (11:25). In addition, there were Simeon (an African), Lucius (perhaps one of the group mentioned in 11:20), and Manaen who was brought up at the court with Herod Antipas (who ruled during the public ministry of Christ). One day as they were serving the Lord, the Spirit said, "Set apart for Me Barnabas and Saul for the work to which I have called them." Two-fifths of the local leadership were being led out into other service.

The church evidently did not hesitate, but after fasting and prayer laid their hands on them (as an indication of their association with them in their future ministry) and sent them away. So the first missionaries departed; and quite naturally they headed for Cyprus, the home of one of them (Barnabas).

EVENTS IN CYPRUS, 13:5–13

Salamis, on the east coast of Cyprus, was the first stop on that island. After preaching there in the synagogues, the group (including John Mark who went along as a helper) went across the island to Paphos. There the Roman deputy of the island, Sergius Paulus, was converted after a struggle with Elymas the sorcerer who tried to keep him from believing. Paul, discerning that Elymas was a tool of the devil, called down temporary blindness on him for his wickedness. It was here too that Paul began to use his Roman name, Paul, since he was now in a Gentile environment. Saul was his Jewish name and Paul his Roman name, and as was the common custom he would have been given both names at birth. Certainly the two names in no way represent the two natures, but simply the particular emphasis of his ministry now to Gentiles caused him to use his Greek name Paul.

Leaving Cyprus the party crossed the Mediterranean to Perga where John Mark decided to leave and return to Jerusalem. No reason is given for his defection, though evidently Paul considered whatever reason it was an unjustified one (15:38).

EVENTS IN GALATIA, 13:14–14:20
Antioch in Pisidia, 13:14–52

Pisidia was one of the regions into which the Roman province of Galatia was divided. Paul and Barnabas came to this region

(3,600 ft. in elevation) after crossing the Taurus Mountains from Perga. As was his custom, Paul went first to the synagogue where he was invited to speak (and this is the longest recorded sermon of Paul's). The message was similar to Stephen's defense.

First there was a historical review (vv. 17–25) extending from the events of the Exodus to the life of David and particularly the promise of a son given to David and finally to John the Baptist who clearly was not the fulfillment of that promise. This gave a natural introduction for the next part of the message, which showed that Christ, David's greater Son, was the fulfillment of that promise. Thus, second, Paul preached the gospel as it is in Jesus Christ to them (vv. 26–39). He was the one who fulfilled "everyone who believes is freed from all things, from which you could not be freed through the Law of Moses" (v. 39). This is a most startling statement, for Paul was saying that the law of Moses could not justify anyone, but Christ offers complete justification to every believer. Third, Paul warned his hearers not to ignore what they had just heard (vv. 40–41). One of the underlying thrusts of this message is this: ignorance of the written Word (the Old Testament prophecies concerning Messiah in this case) leads to ignorance of the living Word. It is so today.

The result of this testimony was that some rejected and some believed, but the whole city heard the Word of God (v. 44). And because of the multitudes who did listen, the Jews were jealous and spoke against Paul and Barnabas. So the missionaries turned their attention to the Gentiles and those who were ordained to (set in the rank of) eternal life believed. But the Jews finally stirred up enough women and leading men to drive Paul and Barnabas to Iconium. But a work of grace had been done and in Gentile hearts largely, and the disciples were filled with joy and the Holy Spirit.

Iconium, 14:1–5

Unbelief is morally vicious. This was illustrated at Iconium where the unbelieving Jews stirred up the Gentiles to divide the people, persecute the apostles, and attempt to drive them from the city. The gospel is indeed a savor of life to some and of death to others (2 Cor. 2:15–16). When the apostles became aware of the intensity of the planned attack, they fled to Derbe and Lystra. Retreat is not always an unworthy procedure particularly when the retreat involves further or different opportunities to witness.

Derbe and Lystra, 14:6–20

At Lystra two important things happened—a miracle and a stoning. The miracle was the healing of a man lame from birth. So stunning was it that when the news spread like wildfire among the people they thought Paul and Barnabas were gods and they prepared to make a sacrifice unto them. When the apostles realized what was happening, they spoke to them in an effort to restrain them. Evidently the reason Paul and Barnabas did not realize what the people were doing was that the people were speaking in their native tongue, Lycaonian, and Paul and Barnabas simply did not understand that particular dialect (even though Paul had the gift of tongues, 1 Cor. 14:19). The speech Paul made on that occasion was a very general statement about the goodness of God, which distinguished Him from all other gods and particularly from Paul and Barnabas who were men. Even at that it was not easy to restrain the people from doing sacrifice.

The second event was the stoning of Paul at the instigation of Jews from Antioch and Iconium. More than one hundred miles separated Antioch from Lystra, yet they dogged Paul's trail and stirred up the people so much that they stoned the apostle. Perhaps Barnabas escaped because he was not the leader. Some feel that Paul was speaking of this experience of stoning in the account of 2 Corinthians 12:1–5, while others think that it was on this occasion that he received the marks spoken of in Galatians 6:17. In any case there is grim irony in the quick reversal of the people's attitude toward the one whom shortly before they thought to be a god! Too, God performed a miracle at Lystra, for Paul got up from the stoning and the next day was strong enough to leave for Derbe. Some believe that the apostle actually died and was raised, while others assume that he was not really dead. Nevertheless, raised or merely revived, it was a miracle that the effects of the stoning did not prevent him from going on so soon to Derbe.

EVENTS ON THE RETURN, 14:21–28

The itinerary of the return trip to Antioch in Syria was a retracing of their steps (with the omission of Cyprus). The work of the return trip was that of confirmation and ordination. Apparently many of the believers in the various cities were suffering persecution and Paul and Barnabas exhorted them to stand fast in the realization that such was normal. Further, they appointed elders in these places so that the infant churches would not be left unorganized (v. 23—the word translated "ordain" means to appoint or designate). Finally they arrived home in Antioch where they made known the blessing of God particularly in opening the door of salvation to the Gentiles as He had so abundantly done on this first missionary journey.

THE COUNCIL AT JERUSALEM

ACTS 15:1–35

....

THE DISSENSION, 15:1–6

As time went on it was inevitable that the problems raised by the presence of Gentiles in the church would come to a head. Peter had learned the lesson of the sheet filled with unclean animals and realized that no man should be called common or unclean—not even Gentiles. At first the Jerusalem church had accepted Cornelius and those converted with him on an equal basis with the Jewish converts and without the necessity of being circumcised. However, as larger numbers of Gentiles came into the blessings of salvation, the numbers of Jewish believers who held that circumcision was necessary for Gentile converts just as it was for Gentile proselytes asserted themselves. Some even came from Jerusalem to Antioch and taught that circumcision and the keeping of the Mosaic law was necessary for salvation. Naturally these Judeans would not fellowship with uncircumcised Gentiles even if they were believers in Christ. This aggravated the matter.

But Paul and Barnabas were discerning enough to see this as not simply a question of fellowship, but one of the fundamental doctrine of salvation by grace versus salvation by works. So they were sent to Jerusalem to try to settle this matter. On the way they declared the conversion of the Gentiles on the first missionary journey to the churches in the cities through which they passed, and when they finally arrived in Jerusalem they found the same doctrine being promulgated by some of the believers who had had a Pharisaical background. Any addition to salvation by grace in any day, whether it be the addition of circumcision or the keeping of the law or anything else, is a problem similar to and equally as serious as the one that faced the Jerusalem council.

THE DISCUSSION, 15:7–18

Before the public discussion, Paul and Barnabas rehearsed privately to the apostles and elders at Jerusalem the things that God had done (v. 4). The public discussion involved much questioning and statements by Peter, Paul and Barnabas, and James. It was logical that the group should hear Peter first since he was the one used of God to open the door of salvation to the Gentiles (vv. 5–11). He simply rehearsed what God had done; then he reminded them that they as Jews could not bear the yoke of the law; and finally he declared that "we [Jews] believe that we are saved [literally] . . . in the same way as they [Gentiles] also are" (v. 11). In other words, salvation is by faith for both groups.

After this Paul and Barnabas added their testimonies as to what God had done on their missionary journey in saving Gentiles (v. 12).

Finally, James, the half-brother of the Lord, the recognized leader of the church at Jerusalem (cf. 12:17; 21:18), summarized matters. After reviewing Peter's testimony that God first visited Gentiles through his ministry, he quoted a prophecy from Amos 9:11–12 as confirming this order of events in God's program. The order is: (1) God visits Gentiles; (2) after this Christ will return;

(3) the millennial kingdom will be established and in it Gentiles will return to the Lord. In other words God has not abandoned His plans for the kingdom of Israel. He will do it after Christ returns, but in the meantime He is calling out from among Gentiles a people for His name.

THE DECISION, 15:19-35

The decision was: "we do not trouble those who are turning to God from among the Gentiles" (v. 19). This means that the council affirmed the principle of salvation by grace. To trouble them would have meant to circumcise them. Not to trouble them meant that circumcision was unnecessary to salvation. This was the unequivocating decision of the council.

Mention was made of the fact that this problem not only affected doctrine but it also affected fellowship between Jewish and Gentile believers. The doctrinal decision was clearly worded that faith alone was necessary for salvation. However, the council made a further suggestion concerning this matter of fellowship. It was simply that the Gentile Christians might well abstain from certain things that would be offensive to Christians with a Jewish background. These were things that were permissible for any believer, but that were repugnant to those with Jewish rearing and that therefore when practiced by Gentile believers were a hindrance to fellowship. They were: things offered in sacrifice to idols (cf. v. 29 where "things contaminated by idols" is explained); fornication (which is probably to be understood in the special sense of breaches of the Jewish marriage regulations listed in Leviticus 18 and not in the general sense of all illicit sexual relations); things strangled in which the blood remained; and from blood (either separate from meat or in the same sense as things strangled).

This decision and suggestion by James was accepted by the others, and they implemented it by writing it in letters and sending the news to the other churches. Paul, Barnabas, Judas, and Silas were delegated to take these letters. Their first stop was Antioch where the news was joyously received and where Silas chose to remain and minister to the church. A potentially dangerous schism in the church had been averted. An important doctrinal matter had been clearly settled, and a suggestion had been made so that Jew and Gentile might live in harmony in the assemblies. Peace had been restored but it was only temporary. Those who taught faith plus circumcision did not accept the decision, for we know that these Judaisers dogged the steps of Paul and persisted in their campaign of forcing the Mosaic law on Gentile converts.

THE SECOND MISSIONARY JOURNEY

ACTS 15:36–18:22

....

THE JOURNEY BEGUN, 15:36–40

The time was approximately the year 50. The place was Antioch in Syria. The scene was one of contention.

The Cause of Contention

When Paul and Barnabas felt that they wanted to return to the churches founded on the first journey, Barnabas wanted to take John Mark with them again. But Paul evidently felt that his returning home from Perga on the first journey was uncalled for, and he refused to take him.

The Continuation of the Contention

The verbs in verses 37–38 are in the imperfect tense indicating that the discussion went on at length.

The Character of the Contention

This was no trivial argument but a sharp contention (v. 39 KJV). The only other use of this word "contention" is in Hebrews 10:24.

The Consequence of the Contention

As a result Paul chose Silas who had been sent with the letters from the Jerusalem council, and Barnabas took John Mark (cf. Col. 4:10). Paul and Silas went overland north through Syria and into Cilicia while the others went back to Cyprus. Apparently the church sided with Paul in this argument (v. 40), but two sets of missionaries went forth because of it.

THE CHURCHES REVISITED, 15:41–16:5

The work of the journey included three things.

Confirming, 15:41

This, of course, was the chief purpose of the journey. There was no thought of going on to new fields, but simply of revisiting the churches that had been founded on the first journey and confirming the disciples in their faith.

Circumcising, 16:1–3

When Paul and Silas came to Lystra they asked a young, reputable disciple to join their party. Timothy was evidently converted through Paul's ministry on the first journey (1 Tim. 1:2). He had a good reputation and was ordained by the church to preach (1 Tim. 4:14; 2 Tim. 1:6). However, Paul thought it wise to circumcise him before he went with them. Timothy was of mixed parentage, his mother being a Jewess and his father a Greek. Therefore, because of his being partly Jewish, Paul thought it best to circumcise him so that he would give no offense to the Jews to whom he might witness. In another instance Paul was very insistent that Titus, a Gentile, not be circumcised (Gal. 2:3).

Communicating, 16:4–5

As they came to the various churches, they reported the decision of the Jerusalem council that salvation is by faith alone and they delivered the letter containing the recommendation about living in harmony. As a result the churches were strengthened in the faith (this is the same word as in 3:7, 16) and were increasing in number daily.

THE VISION ENLARGED, 16:6–11

After preaching in Phrygia and Galatia, the group tried to go into Asia Minor but were forbidden by the Spirit. So they turned north to Bithynia but were again prevented by the Spirit. So they awaited further leading from the Lord in Troas; Asia needed the gospel, but this was not God's time. Need did not constitute their call. They had just come from the east; they had been forbidden to go south or north, but they did not presume that the Lord was leading them to the west—they waited His specific directions. Logic alone is not the basis for a call.

It was at Troas, near the site of ancient Troy, that the Lord gave them that specific leading through the vision of the man of Macedonia. This Greek man represented the finest of civilized and cultured humanity of that day. And yet he lacked the knowledge of the true God, and in his need cried out for help. Immediately the group sought passage across the Aegean to Neapolis (the seaport about ten miles from Philippi). At this point Luke joined the party (notice the "we" in v. 10).

THE WORK AT PHILIPPI, 16:12–40

The ancient name of Philippi was Crenides (from its many springs) until Philip of Macedon seized it and called it after himself. It passed to the Romans with the rest of Macedonia in 168 BC and in its vicinity was fought the battle where Brutus and Cassius were defeated by Antony and Octavian (later the Emperor Augustus) in 42 BC. Then it was made a Roman colony, which was a piece of Rome transplanted abroad. The citizens of Philippi and all Roman colonies enjoyed the same privileges as those in Rome itself. They had the same laws and rights as the Italians. Other such colonies in Acts are Antioch in Pisidia, Lystra, Troas, Ptolemais, and Corinth. Philippi is also called by Luke "the chief city"—a reference to its first-rate importance in population, prominence, and wealth. It was there that the gospel was first preached in Europe.

The Opening of the Work, 16:12–15

Delay and disappointment characterized the first days of the work at Philippi. Paul waited until the Sabbath came and then went to the riverbank in order to preach to the Jews of the city. Apparently there were not available even ten men required for the formation of a Jewish synagogue, for the handful of Jewish women in the city had to meet by the river for prayer. But Paul preached the gospel to them and the Lord opened the heart of Lydia. But what a disappointment that must have been! Paul had been called of the Lord to Europe. He had faithfully preached. The first convert was not only a woman (and men were needed if a church was to be established) but a woman of Thyatira in Asia. Nevertheless, others were also converted—Lydia's household, that is, her servants and dependents, and very likely through Lydia others in Thyatira heard the message when she returned home.

The Opposition to the Word, 16:16–24

Paul and the others continued to witness, and the impact of their testimony was felt throughout the city (vv. 17, 20). Satan then began to work and chose to oppose the testimony by causing a demon-possessed slave girl to follow Paul around for days crying, "These men are bond-servants of the Most High God, who are proclaiming to you the way of salvation." Even though she spoke the truth, it is easy to imagine the damage her cry did to Paul's ministry simply because it would put his true message in the same category in the minds of the people as all her false soothsaying. Finally, Paul, wearied with her, commanded the demon to come out of her. This immediately cut off the source of livelihood for her masters who very cleverly charged the missionaries with speaking treasonous words (v. 21). The magistrates being very conscious of their exalted position as leaders of a Roman colony sought to quell any possible disturbance by beating Paul and Silas, jailing them, and putting their feet in stocks. As a Roman citizen Paul was exempt from beating and ordinary arrest, but he did not make his citizenship known until the next morning. Perhaps he did not have opportunity because of the haste of the magistrates.

The Outcome of the Work, 16:25–40

Because they witnessed, Paul and Silas now found themselves in jail (obviously Timothy and Luke were not involved in this incident). But God was still working, and at midnight while Paul and Silas were singing praises to God, an earthquake opened the doors and loosed the bands of the prisoners. When the keeper of the prison realized what was happening, he, being a Roman soldier and liable for the safety of his prisoners under pain of death, drew his sword to kill himself. But when Paul either saw him silhouetted in the light of the door or heard him draw his sword, he assured him that no one had attempted to escape (perhaps Paul had restrained the other prisoners or they were too stunned by the earthquake to think about making an attempt). In any case the keeper, under great conviction from the previous testimony of the missionaries and the events of that night, asked, "What must I do to be saved?" Paul's classic reply was: "Believe in the Lord Jesus, and you will be saved, you and your household." The words "and your household" must be understood as connected with "believe" as well as "be saved"; that is, his household would be saved if they would believe too. Evidently he and his house did believe for they witnessed to it by baptism that very night.

The next morning the magistrates sent word to let the prisoners go. It was then that Paul spoke of his Roman citizenship and demanded a public discharge by way of an apology for their unlawful acts the preceding day. The magistrates obliged, for they realized that they had treated illegally these citizens of Rome. So they were released, but before departing from the city they called on Lydia; and the ones who had been through the experience of prison comforted the household of Lydia!

THESSALONICA, BEREA, AND ATHENS, 17:1–34

Thessalonica, 17:1–9

In Paul's day Thessalonica was an important city. It was named in 315 BC for and by the wife of Cassander, a stepsister of Alexander the Great; it was the capital of the province of Macedonia with a population of about 200,000; it was an important commercial center and a free city governed by the people (v. 5).

As was his custom, Paul went first to the synagogue and preached that Jesus of Nazareth was the Christ. This he did for three Sabbaths with the result that some Jews, many Gentiles, and several chief women believed. The unbelieving Jews tried to assault the apostles but could only get at their host, Jason. However, they dragged him before the rulers and charged him with harboring people who talked treason by speaking of another king, Jesus. So they took bail from Jason, and apparently he had to agree that Paul would not return to the city and become a public nuisance again (cf. 1 Thess. 2:18).

Berea, 17:10–14

In Berea, forty miles from Thessalonica, the story was repeated —synagogue, witnessing, faith, opposition. There was one difference. It is said that the Bereans were more noble. This may have to do with their class background though it likely means of noble character; that is, free from prejudice, impartial. This was displayed in their being willing to search the Scriptures and test the truth of Paul's message. However, the Thessalonian Jews hounded Paul in Berea with the result that he was forced to leave, though Timothy and Silas remained there. They later joined him in Athens (1 Thess. 3:1–2).

Athens, 17:15–34

While Paul waited for Silas and Timothy, he was stirred by the sights that he saw in Athens. Idols were everywhere, and opportunities for testimony were everywhere. He witnessed in the synagogue and in the marketplace. Shortly his witness became known and the Epicureans (who believed that pleasure was the chief end of life) and the Stoics (who were pantheistic and self-sufficient) took Paul to Mars Hill, in order to hear him further. Areopagus, or Mars Hill, was an Athenian court that met in early times on the Hill of Ares west of the Acropolis. It had jurisdiction over moral questions and religious matters. Paul's message on this occasion was cleverly presented. He began with a kindly ambiguous reference to the religious interest of the people. He next remarked on the fact that they had a statue to an unknown god. Then he proceeded to tell them who that unknown god is. He is the one who is creator, Lord, not confined in temples, preserver, Father of all creation, governor of the nations, and the one in whom we live, move, and have our being (vv. 24–28). Therefore, if He created man, He Himself must be more than a mere man or idol, and He should be listened to when He commands men everywhere to repent. Repentance is imperative too because someday He will judge man by Jesus whom He raised from the dead. With the mention of the resurrection, the crowd became restless, some mocking, others deferring judgment, and at least two (one a judge of the court of Areopagus and the other a woman) were converted.

CORINTH, 18:1–17

Long a commercial and naval rival of Athens, Corinth stood at the junction of important land routes north and south and sea routes east and west. Warships were known to have been built there as long ago as 664 BC; and although it was destroyed at the time of the Roman conquest of Greece in 146 BC, it was restored and given status as a colony by Julius Caesar in 46 BC. It was also made the capital of the province of Achaia in 27 BC. Because of its commercial importance Corinth attracted a number of Jews. It was also notorious because of widespread immorality.

The Missionary, 18:1–11

Paul arrived in Corinth a discouraged man. His missionary activities in Europe had not been well received. Philippi, Thessalonica, Berea, and Athens had all been difficult places of ministry.

Forced to work at his trade of tent making, Paul came in contact with Aquila and Priscilla, Jews who had been evicted from Rome under the edict of Claudius in AD 49. In the midst of this discouraging situation, Paul was encouraged by his friends (v. 5a), by the Word (v. 5b), and by the Lord (v. 10). His friends Silas and Timothy rejoined him and brought him good news of the steadfastness of the Christians in Thessalonica (1 Thess. 3:6). Too, they evidently brought material help (cf. 2 Cor. 11:8; Phil. 4:15). This released him from some financial pressure so that he was able to begin "devoting himself completely to the word." His faithful preaching brought opposition, but the Lord appeared to him in a night vision and assured him that he should stay in Corinth and continue his ministry.

The Ministry, 18:1–11

As has been mentioned, Paul's ministry in Corinth was first to those with whom he worked, Aquila and Priscilla. He also preached in the synagogue every Sabbath, but when the Jews rejected his message he turned to the Gentiles. Nevertheless there were outstanding trophies of grace—Crispus, the ruler of the synagogue, and Justus, a Gentile who lived next door to the synagogue.

The Magistrate, 18:12–17

Gallio was from an illustrious family. His father was the elder Seneca; his brother was Seneca the Stoic and tutor of Nero; and his nephew was Lucan the poet. He became proconsul of Achaia in AD 51 and is characterized in extra-biblical writings as an amiable, witty, and lovable person. When the Jews tried to charge Paul with doing things "contrary to the law," Gallio replied that he was not concerned about Jewish law and that Paul had committed no offense against Roman law. The Greeks took advantage of Gallio's refusal to take the Jews' side in the matter and vented their anger on the Jews by beating Sosthenes who had succeeded Crispus as the chief ruler of the synagogue. Apparently Sosthenes, too, eventually became a Christian (1 Cor.1:1). After these things Paul remained in the city for some time and took advantage of the freedom that Gallio's favorable verdict had afforded him.

THE JOURNEY COMPLETED, 18:18-22

Several noteworthy events occurred on the return to Antioch. First, Paul took Aquila and Priscilla with him as far as Ephesus where they took up residence. Second, he apparently concluded a Nazarite vow and signified it by shaving his head at Cenchrea (the seaport of Corinth). The time and purpose of such a vow was voluntarily determined, though thirty days was the minimum. Third, Paul could not stay in Ephesus very long since he wanted to get to Jerusalem in time for the feast, i.e., Passover. Finally, he landed at Caesarea, went up to Jerusalem, and then returned to the home base in Antioch. Thus the second missionary journey was completed.

THE THIRD
MISSIONARY JOURNEY

ACTS 18:23–21:17

....

EPHESUS, 18:23–19:41

Before describing the ministry of Paul in Ephesus, Luke brings the record up to date by recounting the ministry of Aquila and Priscilla who had remained in Ephesus while Paul returned to Palestine. The entire work at Ephesus, whether through Aquila and Priscilla or through Paul, is a vivid illustration of the power of the Word in hearts and lives.

The Power of the Word in Correction, 18:23–19:7

Ephesus was a city of power. Being the capital of proconsular Asia the citizens were constantly reminded of the power of Rome by the presence of the proconsul. Its location near the mouth of the Cayster River on the main trade route between Rome and the east made Ephesus the greatest commercial center in Asia at that time. It was also a free city with its own Senate and Assembly. But it was the power of Satan that reigned in the city, for at Ephesus stood one of the seven wonders of the ancient world, the temple of Diana. It was a magnificent structure with its 127 columns 60 feet high standing on an area 425 feet in length and 220 feet in width. It was the center of all heathen worship in that area.

Our attention is first drawn to a man named Apollos, an Alexandrian Jew. He had evidently heard some of the facts of the ministry of Christ, but had not known the whole story, particularly the coming of the Spirit at Pentecost. He spoke eloquently in the synagogue but only of the baptism of John the Baptist. Aquila and Priscilla who had been converted under Paul's ministry in Corinth took him aside one day and expounded the Christian message to him more thoroughly. Then he went to Greece being recommended by letter to the churches there. We know that for a time he ministered in Corinth (1 Cor. 1:12). The Word corrected his lack of full understanding of the gospel.

Later, when Paul came to the city, he discovered twelve disciples of John the Baptist, who, like Apollos, knew only the baptism of John the Baptist. He inquired of them if they had received the Holy Spirit when (not since) they believed (v. 2). When they showed ignorance of the Spirit, Paul discovered that they had only known the baptism of John, which pointed to Messiah who was to come and who sent the Spirit. So when they were corrected by the Word as Paul explained it to them (v. 4) they were baptized in the name of the Lord Jesus and received the Spirit. This is the only recorded instance of rebaptism in the New Testament, and it clearly indicates that baptism followed genuine conversion.

The Power of the Word in Conversion, 19:8–10

As was his custom, Paul went to the synagogue and witnessed for three months to the Jews. In due time the gospel had both its saving and hardening effects, and when some became obstinate Paul separated the disciples and taught them in the lecture hall of Tyrannus. Paul probably worked at tent making from daybreak until 11:00 a.m., when Tyrannus would have completed his lectures (cf. 20:34), and then he taught his disciples from 11 until 4 p.m. (as one manuscript adds). This continued for two years during which time those who were being instructed in turn became evangelists so that all those in the district of Asia had heard the Word of the Lord. Not all believed, but all were evangelized through the faithful witness of Paul and the instructed converts.

The Power of the Word in Conviction, 19:11–20

As elsewhere God confirmed at Ephesus the preaching of the Word by signs and miracles. To Paul was given special ability to heal the sick. As a result the reputation of the power of the name of Jesus spread, so that on one occasion seven exorcists from one family tried to use it with disastrous results. They were attempting to cast out a demon from a man and decided to use this new medicine, the name of Jesus. But when they invoked that name the demon asked who they thought they were. Then he came out of the man and tore into the seven exorcists, wounding them and causing them to flee from the house naked. This startling display of the misuse of Jesus' name brought fear to the Christians and conviction of their own misdeeds. Ephesus was known for its magic, and apparently the Christians had not yet put away all such evil practices. So they brought their books and scrolls of magic and burned them as an open repudiation. Then—after the believers made their relationships with the Lord right—the Word of God grew and prevailed (v. 20).

The Power of the Word against Corruption, 19:21–41

As Paul was making his plans to return to Greece and Palestine and then go on to Rome (the first mention of that city in the book

is in v. 21) a riot developed in Ephesus. It was instigated by Demetrius and the others who fashioned small silver shrines, which
people bought to place in dedication at the temple of Diana. Of
course with the conversion of so many people to Christianity,
business had fallen off. So Demetrius organized the whole craft
and incited a general strike. His argument was not that the silver-
smiths' business had declined, but that the Christians were doing
damage to the civic standing and pride of Ephesus by refusing
to worship Diana. This aroused the entire city so that the people
ran to the amphitheater and for two hours cried, "Great is Arte-
mis of the Ephesians!" They had captured Gaius and Aristarchus,
and Paul was about to go himself to try to restrain the crowd,
but the disciples prevented him. Eventually the town clerk, the
executive officer who was an Ephesian and not a Roman and who
was responsible for the good conduct of such meetings, quieted
the crowd by reminding them that actually the Christians had
committed no crime and that the people themselves would be
held accountable by the Romans for such an unlawful assembly.
The Word through changed lives affects the society that those
lives touch.

GREECE, 20:1–5

After this Paul departed to Macedonia. The purpose of this
visit was to collect the contributions of the churches of Macedonia and Achaia for the relief of the poor saints in Jerusalem (cf.
1 Cor. 16:2; 2 Cor. 8–9). He may have spent as long as a year
in Macedonia ("those districts" of v. 2). Then he went south to
Achaia ("Greece" in v. 2 is used as the popular term for Achaia,
the southern part of Greece). There (from Corinth) the epistle
to the Romans was written. He wanted to return to Jerusalem
for Passover, but he learned of a plot against his life (perhaps to

be hatched on board the ship that would take him there) so he returned through Macedonia and sailed from Philippi.

ASIA MINOR, 20:6-38
Preaching to the Believers in Troas, 20:6-12

When Paul came to Troas he met with the believers on Sunday when they gathered to break bread (probably a meal plus the Lord's Supper). He spoke to them until midnight. This was a rare opportunity for the people of Troas to hear the teaching of an apostle. In spite of this, the combination of the lateness of the hour, a long day's work (which many of them would have put in before the evening worship service), the crowd, and the atmosphere caused by the burning of the many lamps, all combined to put Eutychus to sleep and he fell out of the third floor window. According to Dr. Luke the fall killed him (v. 9), but when Paul lifted him up his life returned (v. 11).

Parting with the Elders of Ephesus at Miletus, 20:13-38

Leaving Troas Paul decided to walk the 20 miles to Assos while Luke and the others went by ship. In due time they came to Miletus about 30 miles from Ephesus, and because Paul was in a hurry to get to Palestine he decided not to go to Ephesus but to send for the elders to come to him at Miletus. He had already been thwarted in his plans to be in Jerusalem for Passover and he did not want to miss being there for Pentecost. His remarks to the elders were built along three lines of thought.

First, Paul reminded them of the character of his own ministry (18-27). Evidently Paul's opponents had been attacking him in his absence, so he defended his ministry. It had been characterized by humility of mind, by tears, and by many trials (v. 19). It had been consistently performed publicly and privately (from house to house, v. 20). Its contents had been the preaching of repentance and faith (vv. 21, 24), the kingdom of God (v. 25), and the whole purpose of God (v. 27). Second, Paul gave a charge to the elders (vv. 28-31). It was simply to take care of the church over which God had made them overseers. Notice that the same group who are here called overseers or bishops are also called elders in verse 17 and notice too that in this verse they are said to feed (the same word as pastor) the flock. It seems as if elder, bishop, and pastor are the same. The phrase "with His own blood" in verse 28 should be translated "with the blood of His own [Son]"; i.e., with the blood of Christ. Third, Paul commended them to God (vv. 32–38). It is the word of His grace that is the building and sanctifying agent in any life. Paul concluded with another word of defense of the conduct of his own ministry among them. In verse 35 there is a saying of Christ that is nowhere else recorded in the Scriptures.´ The substance is elsewhere (Luke 6:38; 11:9) but this actual form must also have been well known and widely used. When Paul had finished speaking, the elders reluctantly and sorrowfully took their leave because he had warned them that he would probably see him no more.

PALESTINE, 21:1–17

Tyre, 21:1–6

It was hard, too, for Paul to leave his beloved Ephesian elders (the phrase "parted from them" literally means "tore ourselves away"). He came in due course to Tyre in Phoenicia (cf. 11:19). Evidently he knew none of the believers there, for he had to seek them out. But while the ship was unloading, Paul spent a week with them. He was warned by them under the leading of the Spirit not to go on to Jerusalem, but he felt he must go anyway. So they accompanied him to the ship and said farewell.

Caeserea, 21:7–14

The ship docked briefly at Ptolemais (modern Acre) where Paul apparently left it and traveled overland to Caesarea. There he and his party stayed with Philip the evangelist (8:5) and his four virgin daughters who had the gift of prophecy. Agabus soon appeared on the scene having come from Judea (cf. 11:28) and he through the Spirit prophesied that Paul would be bound and delivered to the Gentiles in Jerusalem. Yet in spite of these warnings the apostle felt he must go on.

Jerusalem, 21:15–17

After several days the group got ready and started on their way. Some of the brethren from Caesarea accompanied them, including an elderly disciple, Mnason, with whom the group stayed in Jerusalem. Perhaps it was from him that Luke received some of the information about the early days of the church in Jerusalem. They finally arrived in Jerusalem and the third missionary journey was completed.

ON TO ROME

ACTS 21:18–28:31

....

DEFECTION IN JERUSALEM, 21:18–26

The story now moves rapidly toward the first confinement in Rome where Luke's chronicle concludes. Back in Jerusalem all was not peaceful. Jewish believers were accusing Paul of forbidding Gentile believers to be circumcised (cf. 16:3). The leaders of the church, while rejoicing in the thousands of Gentiles who had believed through the ministry of Paul, were nevertheless desirous of placating the Jewish Christians. The position of the Gentile believers had been clarified by the letters that the first council had sent (v. 25), but something had to be done to assure the Jewish Christians that Paul was not against the Mosaic law.

James, the recognized leader of the Jerusalem church (apparently none of the twelve apostles was in Jerusalem), and the elders had a proposition all worked out, which they put to Paul. It was simply this: there were four men in Jerusalem whose vow (Nazarite, probably) had come to an end. The rites of purification required before they could shave their heads and thus signify the end of the period of the vow involved a number of offerings. James suggested to Paul that he pay for these offerings and purify himself (even though he was not under a vow at that particular time) with these four men. It is known from Josepheus that such an arrangement was not uncommon at that time. Paul, in his desire to be all things to all men, agreed. Two interesting questions arise. First, where did Paul acquire the money required for this and for his subsequent defenses before the Roman rulers and for the hiring of a house for two years in Rome? Probably his churches contributed to him or perhaps he received some kind of inheritance from his family at this time. Second, was Paul out of the Lord's will in this action? God alone knows the full answer to this, though it would seem that he may have gone too far in his desire to please men. Certainly he had had sufficient warnings not to go to Jerusalem.

DEFENSE BEFORE THE MOB IN THE TEMPLE, 21:27–22:30

Seven days had to elapse before a Nazarite could be purified. At the very beginning of this period (v. 27 reads literally, "when the seven days were going to be fulfilled") some Asian Jews (who before had given Paul trouble, cf. 20:19) thought they saw Trophimus, a Gentile, in the restricted part of the temple with Paul. Gentiles could enter the outer court of the Gentiles, but notices in Greek and Latin barred their entrance into the Inner Court. Once the rumor started, it spread fast. The crowd seized Paul. They dragged him out, beating him in the process. The guards who patrolled the top of the colonnades of the temple saw the riot developing and sent word to their captain who took Paul, bound him, and demanded to know who he was and the cause of this disturbance. Paul identified himself (though not as a Roman citizen at this point) and obtained permission to address the crowd.

Paul was charged with teaching against the people, the law, and the temple. He defended himself by showing that he was a good

Jew but one to whom the Lord appeared, and that that appearance was the valid authority for any changes in his life. It is not unlikely that Luke was in the crowd that heard this defense that day. Paul first elaborated on his condition as a true Jew (vv. 1–5). This he proved by rehearsing the facts of his birth, his education, his zeal for the traditions of the law, and his persecution of the Christians. He then recited the events of the appearance of the Lord to him on the Damascus road (vv. 6–16). Verse 16 should be translated literally as follows:

"Having arisen [aorist participle], be baptized; and wash away your sins, having called [aorist participle] on the name of the Lord." In other words, as the arising precedes the baptism, so calling on the name of the Lord precedes forgiveness. Paul then cited a vision that he received of the risen Lord in the temple in Jerusalem commissioning him to preach to the Gentiles (vv. 17–21). There is no other record of this vision.

The reaction of the mob was to let loose a storm of protest against Paul because of the mention of the word Gentiles. Apparently the captain did not know Aramaic in which Paul was speaking, so he had Paul removed from the scene to be examined. As they prepared to scourge him in order to try to make him confess, Paul appealed to his Roman citizenship, which exempted him from such treatment. The captain then prepared to turn him over to the Sanhedrin for questioning.

DISSENSION IN THE SANHEDRIN IN JERUSALEM, 23:1–10

The session before the Sanhedrin was a stormy one. Paul began by asserting his conscience was clear before God. Ananias, a notoriously unscrupulous high priest appointed in AD 47 and assassinated in AD 66, commanded that Paul should be forcibly silenced. Paul protested with a sharp retort but retracted it when he was informed that it was the high priest against whom he had spoken. Why Paul did not recognize him is not stated. It may have been weak eyesight, or the remark in verse 5 may have been sarcasm. When Paul spoke again he successfully divided the house by stating his own Pharisaical background and his present predicament, which was simply that he was being called in question concerning the hope and resurrection of the dead. This divided the house in such an uproarious way that the captain had to rescue Paul by force or he would have been killed.

DELIVERANCE FROM CONSPIRACY TO CAESAREA, 23:11–35

That night after the explosive session before the Sanhedrin, the Lord graciously appeared to Paul and assured him that he would witness for Him in Rome (v. 11). The next day more than forty Jews banded together under an oath not to eat anything until they had killed Paul. They made their plan known to some of the Sanhedrin, and somehow Paul's nephew heard of it. He in turn informed Paul in prison who sent him to the chief captain who made plans to thwart the conspiracy. This he did by sending Paul under heavy escort that very night to Felix the procurator in Caesarea. He also sent along a letter to Felix stating his belief in Paul's innocence as far as Roman law was concerned and also exalting his own part in the entire matter. (Cf. Tertullus's opposite report in 24:7!) Paul arrived safely, was assured of an early hearing, and confined in the palace built by Herod the Great. It is not recorded whether or not the forty conspirators starved to death!

DEFENSE BEFORE FELIX IN CAESAREA, 24:1–27

The Charge, 24:1–9

In five days the accusers arrived. It was an august group headed by the high priest—a most unusual thing—and it included elders and a hired lawyer, Tertullus. The latter's opening remarks to Felix were filled with flattery calculated to erase any animosity that the Jews and Felix had toward each other. Then he presented the charge against Paul. It was twofold. The political aspect of it was sedition against Rome as a ringleader of the sect of the Nazarenes, and the religious aspect of it was profanation of the temple. To this charge the Jews heartily assented.

Paul's defense, 24:10–21

In his defense Paul categorically denied the political aspect of the charge against him. He reminded Felix that he had been in Jerusalem only twelve days (which is scarcely sufficient time to make arrangements to incite a riot against Rome) and that he had gone there only to worship. He confessed to the accuracy of part of the religious charge, for he admitted belonging to the way that his enemies called heresy and believing in God, the Scriptures, salvation ("hope in God"), and future resurrections. However, he insisted that in the practice of this "heresy" he had been living a life with a "blameless conscience both before God and before men" (v. 16). In addition, Paul emphatically denied that he had started any riot in the temple, for he had been there "neither with multitude nor with tumult." Further, he cited the fact that the Sanhedrin did not find fault in him.

Felix's Decision, 24:22–27

Felix was evidently acquainted with Christianity (v. 22, perhaps from his wife, Drusilla), and although he apparently knew that Paul was innocent of the charges brought against him, he merely adjourned the case because of the presence of the influential delegation of Jews from Jerusalem. The pretense he used was that he wanted to hear Lysias's testimony. However, he gave orders that Paul was to have as much freedom as possible under the circumstances.

For two years Paul was kept in this semi-confinement. During that period Felix and Drusilla interviewed him a number of times concerning his faith. Felix's motive was the hope of a bribe (v. 26), but Paul used the opportunities to witness for Christ. Finally, Festus succeeded Felix, but because Felix needed to court the favor of the Jews he left Paul imprisoned.

DEFENSE BEFORE FESTUS IN CAESAREA, 25:1–27

Festus and Paul, 25:1–12

When Festus came to Jerusalem, the leaders of the Jews brought Paul's case to him, accusing him as before. They further asked Festus to have Paul brought to Jerusalem for trial although they did not tell him that they intended to kill Paul on the way. Perhaps the same band of men who formerly plotted against his life was involved here. However, God was watching over Paul and He used Festus's refusal to transfer Paul to protect him. Festus did promise the Jews that he would go to Caesarea and see to the matter. When he did, they accompanied him and accused Paul again. Paul persisted in asserting his innocence of both treason against Caesar and of breaking the Jewish law by profaning the temple. Festus did not want to release Paul because he too wanted to ingratiate himself with the Jews, so he proposed to Paul that he go to Jerusalem to stand trial. At this point Paul reminded Festus that Caesarea was the proper place for the trial (v. 10), that Festus knew he was not guilty (v. 10), and that he would prove to all that he was innocent by appealing to Caesar (v. 11). When Paul saw that Festus was anxious to make concessions to the Jews, he feared that his trial would no longer be conducted impartially; therefore he appealed to Caesar. This right of appeal was an ancient and highly cherished right of Roman citizens, dating back to 509 BC. It could be invoked after a verdict had been given by a lower official, or it could be invoked earlier in the proceedings as in this instance. But when it was invoked it guaranteed that the investigation would be transferred directly to Rome and the verdict rendered by the Emperor himself (who at this time was Nero). Paul may have used this right of appeal to Caesar in order to settle once and for all the question of whether or not Christianity was a legitimate religion independent of Judaism. In any case Festus was quite relieved to be taken off the hook with the Jews.

Festus and Agrippa, 25:13–27

Festus was on the spot for he had to make a report of Paul's case and he realized that he was innocent. His situation was relieved somewhat by the routine visit of Agrippa and Bernice (this is the son of Herod Agrippa I of chapter 12). Festus rehearsed the events that led to Paul's appeal to Caesar and reaffirmed his belief in Paul's innocence as far as Roman law was concerned. Agrippa's interest was aroused and he asked to hear Paul, which arrangements Festus was only too glad to make. The next day Paul was brought to the chamber amid much pomp, and Festus asked Agrippa to examine him in order that he, Festus, might have a definite charge to include in the letter to Caesar. "Perhaps they looked upon him with pity as they saw the chain. But more pity must have filled the heart of the great servant of Christ as he saw the poor lost souls bedecked with the miserable tinsel of earth" (A. C. Gaebelein, *The Acts of the Apostles*, p. 401).

DEFENSE BEFORE AGRIPPA IN CAESAREA, 26:1–32

Having appealed to Caesar, Paul was not actually required to defend himself before Agrippa. Nevertheless he seized upon the opportunity to witness to this Jewish king. This was a remarkable speech, for in it Paul showed great tact and courtesy, yet he was pointed and truthful. There are at least four personal appeals to the king himself (vv. 2, 13, 19, 27).

His pre-conversion life, 26:1–11

First Paul spoke of his life as a zealous Pharisee. Sincerity, not hypocrisy, was the keynote of his life. Because he was a sincere Pharisee he tried to live a blameless life (vv. 4–5), he believed in the promises God made to the Jews (v. 6), and he persecuted zealously the heretical sect of the followers of Jesus (vv. 9–11). All of these things were quite consistent with a sincere Pharisaical life, but they show how sincerely wrong a man can be. The phrase "cast my vote" in verse 10 may be used officially (showing Paul was a member of the Sanhedrin and thus married) or it may be used unofficially (meaning that he was not).

His Conversion, 26:12–18

Paul then proceeded to show that his subsequent change of life could only be explained by what happened on the road to Damascus. It was there that he recognized Jesus of Nazareth as the Messiah and fulfiller of the promises made to the fathers. It was there, too, that Paul was commissioned to go to the Gentiles "to open their eyes so that they may turn from darkness to light and from the dominion of Satan to God, that they may receive forgiveness of sins and an inheritance among those who have been sanctified by faith in Me" (v. 18).

His post-conversion life, 26:19–23

Paul's subsequent life was one of obedience to the commission given him at his conversion. Once again he reiterated the gospel to this distinguished audience (vv. 22–23).

The Verdicts, 26:24–32

Festus interrupted to pronounce his own verdict by saying that Paul was mad. Paul answered him soberly and reasonably—in exactly the opposite way from a madman. Paul then turned to Agrippa since he noticed that the Lord was bringing conviction to his heart and addressed a direct question to the king: "Do you believe the Prophets?" If Agrippa said no, then his reputation for orthodoxy would have vanished. If he said yes, then he would have been in the position of agreeing publicly with Paul's argument. It was one thing to have an academic interest in what Paul was saying; it was quite another thing to confess Christ publicly. So Agrippa passed the question off by replying, "In a short time you will persuade me to become a Christian" (v. 28). Again Paul very solemnly answered with a play on the words "in a short time": "I would wish to God, that whether in a short or long time [i.e., with a few or with many words, with ease or with difficulty], not only you, but also all who hear me this day, might become such as I am, except for these chains" (v. 29). With this the king arose, signifying the end of the audience. Afterward he declared Paul's innocence (cf. 23:29; 25:25).

DEPORTATION TO ROME, 27:1–28:16

This chapter is one of the most descriptive pieces of literature in the New Testament, corresponding to the first chapter of Jonah in the Old Testament. A sea voyage was not something looked forward to by the ancients. Incommodious ships, the probability of long delays, and the possibility of shipwreck did not make the anticipation of a voyage a pleasure. In this instance, Paul left Palestine in August or September and did not arrive in Rome until March, having lost his ship and his belongings in the meantime.

Caesarea to Myra, 27:1–5

Paul was delivered over to Julius, a centurion, for the trip to Rome. Luke again joined him (notice the "we" in v. 2). At Sidon Paul was allowed to visit his friends, for as a Roman citizen he was to be treated courteously and considered innocent until judged otherwise by Caesar. They then sailed to the east and north of Cyprus to Myra on the southern coast of Asia Minor where Paul and the others were trans-shipped to a vessel from Egypt.

Myra to Crete, 27:6–8

At Myra the party found a ship coming from Alexandria and bound for Rome. They embarked and sailed with difficulty to Fair Havens, a small bay on the southern coast of Crete.

Crete to Malta, 27:9–26

Time was quickly passing and soon the sea would be closed to all shipping. Luke notes that the fast was already past, which refers to the Day of Atonement. This means that it was already October and the sea would be completely closed to all navigation by November. Even then it was dangerous to set sail. Paul warned

Julius but the centurion preferred to believe the captain of the ship; so they set sail. They hoped at least to be able to spend the winter in Phenice, which was a good harbor on the south coast of Crete. Fair Havens was too exposed. But as they sailed along the coast, a wind caught them and they could do nothing but let the ship run with it. They hauled in the dinghy, which was normally towed at the stern (v. 17); they undergirded the ship with cables to strengthen it; and lowered the mainsail. The next day they lightened the ship, and the day following they jettisoned the ship's gear with their own hands (vv. 18–19). (Later even the cargo was cast overboard, v. 38.)

At this point Paul spoke up. He reminded them that he had warned them not to leave Crete, but he assured them that no life would be lost because an angel from God had told him so. He also predicted that they could be cast up on some island.

The Shipwreck, 27:27–44

On the fourteenth night of the storm this came to pass. By taking soundings they realized that they were approaching land and so they dropped the anchors and waited for daylight so that they might get ashore safely (v. 29). In the meantime practical Paul encouraged all aboard to eat something since they had not eaten for the entire two weeks. At daylight they cut loose the anchors and headed the ship toward the shore, but running aground in a narrow channel the ship began to break up (v. 41). The sailors wanted to kill the prisoners, but Julius would not permit it. Instead those who could swim were ordered to jump overboard while the others followed using planks from the ship to help them get to shore safely. In this way all were saved, though the ship was lost, exactly as Paul predicted. Throughout the entire voyage Paul's presence of mind and ascendancy to a place of leadership, though a prisoner, were remarkable. Too, the hand of God controlling every wind, wave, officer, and sailor was evident. All circumstances were under His loving control.

Malta, 28:1–11

Although three months (November, December, and January) were spent on Malta, only two events during that time are recorded. The first occurred immediately on landing. As the people were building a fire and Paul was helping them, a snake bit him. (The word "natives" in v. 2 does not mean uncivilized but rather non-Greek and it is used from Luke's viewpoint.) Although there are no poisonous snakes there now, apparently there were in that day, for the Maltese expected Paul to become ill or even die. But when he did not, they said he was a god.

The second event was the healing of Publius's father. Publius was the chief man in the island, and his father suffered from a fever and dysentery (v. 8). After prayer and the laying on of Paul's hands he was healed. As a result others consulted Paul and Dr. Luke (note the "us" and "we" in v. 10). Evidently some were healed supernaturally and others through the medical means at Luke's command. Quite properly those healed paid their physician. After three months the group boarded another ship from Alexandria for Rome.

Malta to Rome, 28:12–16

From Malta they sailed to Syracuse in Sicily, then to Rhegium on the toe of Italy, and finally to Puteoli in the Bay of Naples. Puteoli was the principal port in Southern Italy and a chief port for discharging grain from Egypt. It is not surprising to read that there were Christians there, with whom Paul stayed for a week. The brethren in Rome also heard of his arrival and traveled the forty-three miles from Rome to Appii Forum on the Appian Way to meet him. This was a great encouragement to the apostle. Finally he arrived in Rome itself, and was delivered by Julius to the captain of the guard though he was permitted relative freedom.

DETENTION IN ROME, 28:17–31

Paul did not waste any time beginning his ministry in Rome, and he followed the usual pattern of witnessing to the Jews first and then the Gentiles (cf. Rom. 9:1–2; 10:1). During his first interview with the leaders of the Jewish community in Rome, Paul simply testified of his innocence. They replied that they had heard nothing of his case but that they would be willing to hear him again concerning the Christian Way. The fact that they had had no word from the Jews in Palestine concerning Paul's case seems to indicate that Paul's persecutors had decided not to prosecute the case further, probably because they realized that Caesar would pronounce Paul not guilty. By not showing up in Rome to prosecute they would simply let the case go by default, and Roman law would keep Paul there more than eighteen months before he could be judged innocent by default. In this way Paul would be kept out of circulation and yet the Jews would not risk allowing Christianity to be judged a non-treasonous religion. (Cf. W. M. Ramsay, *The Teaching of Paul in Terms of the Present Day,* pp. 346–71.)

During the second interview Paul spoke in more detail concerning the Lord Jesus. Some agreed with him and some did not. As they began to depart, Paul reminded them of the prophecy of Isaiah that their hearts would be hardened on hearing the truth. He would then be free to turn to the Gentiles with the message, which he did as much as the relative freedom of confinement in his own hired house permitted. Paul may have been kept out of circulation for these two years, but he was certainly not kept silent.

Why does the Acts stop at this point? I suppose we would ask that question no matter where Luke had chosen to conclude his story. Although we may not fully comprehend his purpose, whatever it was, apparently Luke considered it completed with Paul's arrival in Rome, and thus he felt free to close his record. (For a fuller discussion of Luke's purposes, see the author's *Biblical Theology of the New Testament*, pp. 103–107.) Further, he may have used this two years time to finish the writing of Acts and he may have wished to issue it even before Paul was released. At any rate Luke was satisfied that his purpose had been fulfilled, for he had recorded some of the things that the risen Jesus Christ had continued to do (cf. 1:1), and there is no conclusion to that story.

STUDY THE BIBLE WITH PROFESSORS FROM MOODY BIBLE INSTITUTE

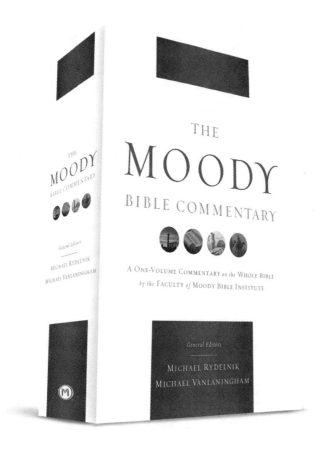

MOODY Publishers®

From the Word to Life®

Study the Bible with a team of 30 Moody Bible Institute professors. This in-depth, user-friendly, one-volume commentary will help you better understand and apply God's written revelation to all of life. Additional study helps include maps, charts, bibliographies for further reading, and a subject and Scripture index.

978-0-8024-2867-7 | also available as an eBook

Dig Deep Into the Whole New Testament!

MacArthur New Testament Commentary Series

The set includes:

Matthew (4 volumes)	Galatians	Hebrews
Mark (2 volumes)	Ephesians	James
Luke (4 volumes)	Philippians	1 Peter
John (2 volumes)	Colossians & Philemon	2 Peter and Jude
Acts (2 volumes)	1 & 2 Thessalonians	1-3 John
Romans (2 volumes)	1 Timothy	Revelation (2 volumes)
1 Corinthians	2 Timothy	Index
2 Corinthians	Titus	

MOODY
Publishers®

*From the Word **to** Life*®

This bestselling 34-volume hardcover commentary set features verse-by-verse interpretation and rich application of God's Word. Easy to understand, yet rich in scholarly background.

978-0-8024-1347-5 | also available as an eBook

ENCOUNTER GOD. WORSHIP MORE.

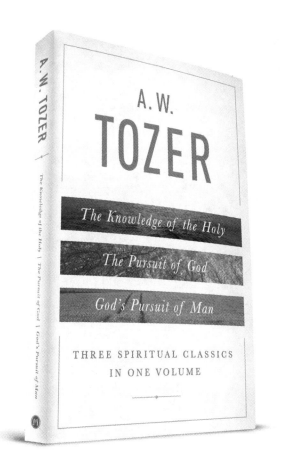

Considered to be Tozer's greatest works, *The Knowledge of the Holy*, *The Pursuit of God*, and *God's Pursuit of Man* are now available in a single volume. In *Three Spiritual Classics*, you will discover a God of breathtaking majesty and world-changing love, and you will find yourself worshipping through every page.

978-0-8024-1861-6